IT'S YOUR LIFE

Inspirational messages to meet the practical problems of life

※※※

By A. REUBEN GORNITZKA

※※※

Publishers

T. S. DENISON & COMPANY

Minneapolis

Printed in the U.S.A.

By The Brings Press

International Copyright Secured

Library of Congress Catalog Card Number: 58-7285

DEDICATION

Dedicated with love to my wife, Ruth, whose inspiration, constructive criticism and skilled assistance helped to make this book possible.

Contents

Introduction

THIS BOOK HAS been written with the hope that you will find inspiration and a spur toward spiritual growth from reading these messages. Each chapter has been written in brief form to provide some "thought-starters" for the busy reader with an anticipation that they may carry your thinking far beyond the last paragraph of the topics discussed.

The writer does not pretend that any of these "thought-provokers" treats the particular theme either fully or adequately. This is true whether it be in reference to breadth or depth, either spiritually or philosophically, of the subject matter. My approach has rather been that of a Christian friend thinking out loud with you about God, man, and the world around us, and with the hope that what is said will help to lead us back to the One, Christ Jesus, in whom man finds his restored relationships both to God and his fellow men.

The everyday world holds many stimulating things within it. It is like a little boy's pockets crammed with so much that is ordinary, but representing to the boy's imaginative mind a whole series of adventures, both past and future. So, likewise, for the Christian with an imaginative mind, each day becomes one of great adventure. In the shoddiest of settings, he may see a thing of beauty in the smudged face of a smiling child. In the wrinkled face of an old woman he may see a "Mary" of the Kingdom. In a lilac blossom he may see Spring in the heart of God.

Whatever it may be, we ought to be seeing something in

God's world which tells us about Him—His power, His love, His beyond-the-infinite variety in persons and peoples, or places and things which cry, "God has been here."

"It's Your Life!" It can be a dull picket-line before God's workshop of life—clambering for better pay, complaining of scrubby treatment, snarling at the boss. By contrast, it can be a creative experimental laboratory in God's amazing world where love outwits hatreds, kindness melts cynicism, and truth routs fear.

The secret of adventure in such a life is Jesus Christ. Of course, it's your life, yours to deal with as you wish, or yours to invest in a full and abundant life. You will invest it in *life* when you say with Paul, "For me to live, is Christ!"

If you find inspiration in the content of this book, I shall be pleased. If a reading of this book should draw your heart closer to your Lord's, I shall be humbly grateful.

—A. Reuben Gornitzka

To Shoot Or To Kneel

WHAT DO YOU do with a choice between a miserable conscience and confession? Very recently a young farmer made his choice and you perhaps caught it in the news. Let me recap this Good Friday news story for you.

A repentent young farmer, whose conscience forced him to confess a break-in of some years ago, is at peace today with himself and the world and his God. About nine years ago when the farmer was a teen-ager, he and another boy stole about six hundred dollars worth of merchandise from a hardware store in Mankato, Minnesota. Two years later he became, the news story said, "serious about his religion." But, he said, every time he knelt to pray his conscience reminded him he had stolen and had not made restitution. Eventually he discussed the matter with his pastor, who urged him to make things right with God. The minister agreed to take the farmer's first payment of fifty dollars to the hardware store.

A few days later the pastor called at the hardware store. The proprietor declined the payment and suggested that the money be given to the church. He left the amount to the pastor's judgment. He said further that he did not want to know who the farmer was but wrote a note for the pastor to deliver. The hardware man wrote: "Your frankness and moral conscience indicate you are entering a future life of strength and godliness. I am not interested in recovering damages." The pastor said the farmer was overcome upon reading the note. He said, "It's like taking our sins to God and being forgiven."

Now here was a remarkable story for a Good Friday release, was it not? A story which has been repeated in many varied forms more times perhaps than anyone but a minister or priest would believe. And it reminds me of another story, this one told by Henrik Pontoppidan from "Peter, the Adventurer." In this story a young man had seduced a young lady in the village and had hurried her off into the mountains to escape from the wrath of the angry villagers. As they climbed the side of the mountain and moved along the twisting paths, they came to a turn in the path where they were confronted by a crucifix. Very quickly the young man reached down, pulled a revolver from his holster and began to shoot.

An apt illustration, is it not? Either we shoot in an attempt to rid ourselves of an accusing conscience or we kneel to find forgiveness and a restored relationship. The wonder of Good Friday and its message is that there is a God who loves and who in Christ forgives in order that a man can be free again.

"When I declared not my sin, my body wasted away . . .

For day and night thy hand was heavy upon me;
 my strength was dried up as by the heat of summer.

I acknowledged my sin to thee . . .
 then thou didst forgive the guilt of my sin."

"Blessed is he whose transgression is forgiven, whose sin is covered."

A Place of
Beginning Again

ONE MIGHT well wonder how it must feel to be one of the Japanese leaders following the event which transpired in a recent Security Council session of the United Nations. What a long road back to that hour when it was recommended that Japan be admitted to membership in the United Nations organization! As it was expected, the General Assembly unanimously adopted this recommendation and made Japan the 80th member of the U.N.

Now as I have thought about Japan's history of recent years, the ugly war with an incendiary Pearl Harbor, the hatreds, the animosities, the bitterness and rancor directed at Japan, and their own economic chaos as a result—I have tried to find a phrase descriptive of this new experience for them. Perhaps it is because they found "a place of beginning again."

That is really what this amazing comeback on the part of Japan suggests to us, is it not? Driven back to its shores, bombed atomically into final submission and defeat, this nation in a very realistic sense stood at a point of a permanent defeatest attitude, or at a point of beginning again. It chose the latter.

And the result? Your newspaper will remind you editorially that Japan today leads the whole world in shipbuilding, ranks third in cotton and textile production, sixth in steel production, and has the highest standard of living in its history. Japan, in spite of its bitter mistakes, its life destroying ambitions in World War II—found its opportunity of beginning again, and capitalized on it. Creditably done, it has found itself voted into U.N. membership.

Individuals as well as nations find themselves needing an opportunity point of "beginning again."

The struggling artist, disappointed in his latest work, discards it and approaches the canvas again with new hope in his heart. The musician, with his most recent composition rejected, seats himself once again at the piano, picks out a new theme and melody, and records his creation on paper. The writer drops his fifth attempt into the well-filled wastebasket and slips a new sheet of paper into the typewriter—and begins again!

But "the place of beginning again" is not alone reserved for the artist, the musician, and the writer in their creative efforts. It is open as well to every last one of us as mortal beings who have failed, who have known our defeats, who have sinned first against God and also against society. We, too, can know something better than defeat and hopeless finality in our spiritual lives. True, our fellow men may often move slowly in granting to us the new opportunity—the opportunity to live down the past and begin again. But God does give us this chance. And from Old Testament days to modern times, society finds itself composed of men and women who through a forgiving God know what it means to come out of defeat into a new life and a new world—a new beginning!

There is a certain sense in which every one of us every day both need and can find the opportunity of beginning again. I need it. I suspect you do, too. The opportunity is ours to claim.

Japan went down to defeat, disgraced before the whole world. Politically and economically, it arose out of the ashes to new days.

Out of the ashes of your "today"—you, too, spiritually, can rise again to a new day tomorrow. The way is through Christ who came into the world to create a new people through repentance and a new faith.

A Cord Through Chaos

DO YOU remember the occasion when Mantle was aiming to duplicate Babe Ruth's home-run record? What tremendous pressure he must have lived under! Here was pressure not only on the part of those wonderful fans of his, the millions who wanted him to break that record, but also pressure on the part of the opposition who wanted to win their ball games, irrespective of Mickey Mantle's record.

Well, while millions have been interested in the pressure under which Mantle lived, perhaps not too many are concerned about the pressure that is yours or mine. But every one of us lives under some kind of pressure. It may be pressure that is known to a good number of folks or it may be pressure that is known only to you. And with it comes the question, "What am I going to do with it?" or "How am I going to handle it?"

Admiral Byrd put this on record when he wrote about his experiences years ago down in Antarctica. He had gone out from the crew base to spend some time making certain scientific tests in a little shack in the icy wilderness. A couple of problems confronted him: The one was trying to keep his sanity because he was all alone; the other was trying to keep his physical vigor because he was fearful of going any distance from the little shack—afraid that he might be suddenly enveloped in an icy snowstorm, or that darkness might fall and he would lose his way.

One day he found an answer. In his equipment he discovered that he had two stakes and a long piece of cord. He stepped out of the door of the shack, planted one stake in the ice, tied one end of the cord to it, walked out as far as the cord would reach and planted the other stake in the ice. He then tied the other end of the cord to that stake. Then, if it were daylight or darkness, if it were clear or snowing, he could slip his fingers in a loop over that cord, walk out and back again as many times as he wanted to without fear, without a possibility of getting lost. Byrd called that cord "a thin cord through chaos."

Faith is like that—sometimes a "thin cord" but better yet, a "stout cord through chaos." Mickey Mantle had to have faith in *himself* that he was going to be able to pound out that ball in order to break any records, or achieve what he did— to win the Most Valuable Player Award. Yes, faith in yourself is important but, more than that, you must have faith also in *your fellow men*. We need that faith, although we are often disappointed by those who surround us.

Faith in yourself is important. Mickey Mantle will not break any records without it. Faith in your fellow men is important. No team player will break records all alone. But important as these faiths are, there is yet another which alone can give these substance. This is faith in the Almighty Creator God.

"I believe, help thou mine unbelief," said one and we, too, point to Him for faith for He is both Saviour and Lord, who put us into this world, who sustains life, who keeps us going. He makes it possible for us to know that we do not walk alone, that we have someone who cares. Christ made that clear. He told us that we are more important than the lilies of the field and the fowl of the air and the fish of the sea.

God cares! Here is the supreme source of faith.

Well, more power to Mickey Mantle for what he was able to do under pressure and, friend, more power to you, too. You, too, live under pressure and with a living faith you will come through it.

"I Got A Glory"

I LOVE SHIPS and I am intrigued by them, just as some of you are, in spite of the fact that I do not own even a row-boat. But seeing a beautiful ship, or crossing the Great Lakes, or trafficking through Puget Sound in Seattle, or circling Manhattan on a ferry boat, intrigues me. And, it reminds me of a little incident in the life of Archibald Rutledge.

Rutledge was aboard an old stern-wheeler on the lower Mississippi. It was a common occurrence for him to wander about the ships he rode to look over the captain's bridge or the engine room, covering the ship like an inspector. Then one day what a surprise! His eyes widened as he stood in the doorway to the engine room. Here, where in the past he had usually found a dirty, greasy hole, he now looked at the most shining, the most sparkling engine room he had ever seen. Even the floor was so clean you could "almost eat off it." "What's happened?" he thought, and then he spied someone to whom he could ask the question. An old Negro engineer sat on a stool in that engine room humming a tune and whittling on a stick of wood. Rutledge asked his question and this was the answer, coming in a cozy drawl: "Well, suh, you see, suh, Ah got a glory."

Here was an engineer who wanted to be just an engineer, not governor of the state, not chairman of a board, not even captain of the ship, just the best engineer on any ship on the Mississippi. "Ah got a glory!" Well, friend, how about you? In your life, is there something of value, of meaning, of worth, that makes life worth living? The Master, Jesus

Christ, had that glory. He spoke of it too. I almost wonder if the Negro engineer had not borrowed his words from John, Chapter 17. It is here that Christ in His prayer speaks of the glory of the Father—the glory that was His as Saviour of the world. Then speaking of His followers, he added in His prayer: "The glory which Thou gavest Me I have given them."

I wonder if Berton Braley had taken Rutledge's story of the engineer and then wrapped it around that prayer of Christ's in order to produce this bit of verse. Listen to it, if you will:

Ya' gotta get a glory in the work you do,
A hallelujah chorus in the heart of you.
Paint, or tell a story; sing, or shovel coal.
But ya' gotta get a glory or your job lacks soul.

The men whose shining armor make our pulses throb
Were the men who got a glory in their daily job.
The vision might be gory and the odds unfair,
But the men who got a glory never knew despair.

O Lord, give me a glory; Is it much to give?
For ya' gotta get a glory or ya' just can't live.

When you get a glory, it is like the sun—
And you can see it shining in the work you've done.
Fame is transitory, riches fade away;
But when ya' get a glory, it is there to stay!

O Lord, give me a glory and a workman's pride
'Cause ya' gotta get a glory or you're dead inside.

Friend, get a glory! God in Christ can give that to any man.

A Wider Vision

IT IS a New Year that we have begun. What lies within it not one of us knows. But we have our hopes, our dreams, our aspirations—and chances are that many of them will be fulfilled.

I hope, however, that your hopes, dreams and aspirations are large enough and wide enough to make their fulfillment worthwhile.

Yesterday I ran across a story written by the Rev. Ensworth Reisner some time ago. In it he tells of a woman he knew who had cataracts on her eyes which had gradually narrowed her vision to a thin point of light. Surgery and the removal of these cataracts enabled her eyes to see the wide horizons again; and this was her statement: "You have no idea how much difference it makes to have wide vision."

There is much truth in that in our work-a-day world: For the football passer in a bowl game, for the driver at an intersection, for the scientist in his laboratory, but beyond that, too.

It must have been such a thought in more than a physical way that William Lyon Phelps had in mind. In his *Autobiography of Letters,* he says: "In my life of professional teaching I have never endeavored to make men more efficient. I have tried to make them more interested. If one is interested, one is usually interesting. The business of the teacher is not to supply information; it is to raise a thirst. I like to hang pictures on the walls of the mind; I like to make it possible for a man to live with himself, so that he will not be bored with himself. For my own part, I live every day as if this were the first day I had ever seen and the last I were ever going to see."

That is wide vision. We need it, every one of us. And we can have it, rich or poor. I have known those of great wealth who have not had it. One day I sat chatting with a wealthy industrialist. In the course of our visit he said to me: "You know, I'm bored to death." Sounds peculiar, doesn't it? "Bored to death" when there was scarcely anything that he could not buy. But he had no vision. Life was all wrapped up in his own little world—a vision narrowed to a thin point of light.

By contrast, I have seen wide horizons in folks who owned very little of this world's goods. I remember an elderly lady who lived in an old folks' home. There she had the constant and wearing care of an aged husband in ill health whose mental abilities had slipped a good deal. But never did I find her anything but radiant. She was everlastingly doing something for someone else. It might be the simplest little thing with nothing of real material value involved—yet the value that it had for those who surrounded her could not be measured. Hers was a wide vision.

A certain woman once went to see a famous psychotherapist, tells John Trevor Davies. The doctor said at the first interview, "Now tell me all about yourself." She needed no second invitation. At the end of an hour the doctor said, "That will do now. I'll see you again tomorrow." The same formula was repeated several times. Then one day the doctor said to the patient, "Madam, I can do no more for you. I advise you to take the first train to Niagara Falls, and there take a long, lingering look at something bigger than yourself." She needed new vision.

You and I do, too, for this coming year. We have our hopes, our plans, our dreams for the coming days, but let us be sure they are the ones that grow out of a wide enough vision to make their fulfillment worthwhile. Then tomorrow will be worth being lived—including you—and God—and your fellowmen—and the result will be a better world. The Apostle Paul had wide vision—his life and work proved it. He said, "it is not I that live, but Christ lives within me."

Owned or Loaned?

A TELEPHONE CALL, a news report — and suddenly you are catapulted into a vacuum. Some friend or loved one will not be around any more. Death has come. This, we have thought, is the kind of thing that can happen to someone else. But now it has happened to us. Life is like that. You may be able to deal rather casually with the death announcement when the name is strange. But you cannot be casual when it is someone you love.

How are we to handle this in our thinking? Can we deal with it sanely? Can we approach this loss with any meaningful kind of understanding? I believe we can. The following story may help to point up the answer.

An Oriental king had a particular love for flowers. One day he called in his head gardener from out of the palace grounds, handed him an unusually beautiful lily plant, and said, "I wish you would take this out into the gardens, dig it down, plant it, water it and care for it as though it were your very own. I want you to love it as I love it." The gardener was very pleased to accept this responsibility from the king. He watched over that lily plant and cared for it as though it were his very own.

The weeks and months passed by until one day he noted that this plant was ready to bloom again. Early the next morning he went out into the garden with great anticipation, expecting to see the plant in its full beauty. To his great disappointment it was gone. A feeling of tragedy came over

24

him. He had been robbed. As he stood there crushed, one of his aides came to his side. The aide told the gardener that early in the morning the king himself had come out into the garden and had discovered his favorite lily plant in full bloom. Having discovered this, he dug it up with his own hands, potted it and took it back into the palace.

The disappointment that had been in the heart of the gardener disappeared. He realized that he had not been robbed at all. The plant had not really been his own. It had only been entrusted to him to care for, to water, to cultivate and to cherish; yet all the while it belonged to the king.

Did you ever stop to think that this is the kind of attitude that we as Christians can take when we lose a loved one? Any of us who has been through this experience knows that it is not an easy one. There are tears and there is sadness. There is a feeling of loneliness and emptiness because a chair is vacant that has been filled over the years.

But is it not true that none of our loved ones really belong to us in the sense that we own them? They belong to the King of Kings and the Lord of Lords who gave them life, who was good enough to entrust these loved ones to our care for us to love, to share life, to share thoughtfulness and courtesy, winsomeness and unselfishness. He gave us the privilege and opportunity of making life richer for them as they have enriched life for us.

And when they are gone we have not been robbed, for they have been taken by the King to whom they always really belonged. He has taken them into the eternal palaces, and we can but say "thank you" for the privilege that was ours, for awhile, of caring for them and of loving them.

How Are You Read?

I SAT in my office one day looking at my personal library. Several thoughts occurred to me as I did so. The hundreds of books in any library tell an often unvoiced story. The covers may be new or old, attractive or unattractive in appearance. The titles may be catchy and to the point, or just words that attract little interest. The names of the authors may be well-known or little known and quite unfamiliar, but these books represent something very real. Here are the ideas of men and of women put down on paper after arduous toil. Some of these ideas and thoughts are old and have been merely restated in a more colorful or understandable way. Some of them are new, dynamic and warm. They almost breathe life to the reader.

Behind the writer is a life, perhaps more interesting and exciting than one might dream or more drab and monotonous than one might imagine. Books represent human personalities behind them, lives lived, ideas dreamed, thoughts put into print — by people.

People, individual human personalities, are important! Like a set of books on a shelf, we may look at people with some disinterest. All we may visibly see are the covers, the jackets, inside of which people live. These physical covers may be attractive or unattractive to the eye or may be seen with some disinterest. But people have souls and minds as well as bodies. These souls are the houses in which they really live and they are God-loved, Christ-bought. They count be-

26

fore God in many ways that cannot be measured.

People are God-created beings, the highest form of His creation, as He has so clearly stated. They are eternal souls with God's eternal Spirit breathed into them, and they are loved by Him, every last one of them. Calvary and Easter are God's most expressive displays of love. But is this what we see and understand—you and I—about ourselves and about other people? Is this the way in which we deal with them? Does this color our relationships to them as we touch their lives, however lightly or however firmly?

By the grace of God we ought to seek constantly to develop the warmest kind of fellowship possible. This should be true in our Sunday worship experience as friendly "hellos" and introductions ought to replace our shyness. The warm acceptance of new members into our church and community group-life ought to become the happily expected. Every day of the week should see this spirit reflected.

A little boy on the street was chatting one day with an interested stranger who, among his other inquiries, asked, "And where do you go to Sunday School, Sonny?" "I go right down there at the corner," said the little boy. "You know, they really love a little fellow down there."

Perhaps there is nothing that will put an attractive "jacket" on the book of your life quite as effectively as a life of kindness toward others. Unnumbered people are yearning for just the warmth of little kindnesses on the part of those around them. Your act of kindness may change another's entire day—perhaps even a lifetime.

One man's reply to the question, "How have you made it through so difficult a life?" was as simple as this, "I had a friend."

Paul said, ". . . Be kind to one another, tenderhearted, forgiving one another, as God in Christ forgave you." We are to be "letters of recommendation . . . to be known and read by all men." We should show that we are a letter from Christ "written not with ink but with the Spirit of the living God, not on tablets of stone but on tablets of human hearts."

Sit On Your Baggage

JAMES TRUSLOW ADAMS records a rather interesting incident that occurred some years ago in the Amazon region of South America. A group of American hunters were moving in a safari through the jungles, accompanied by a group of natives who, by their very nature and physical make-up, were capable of carrying heavy loads and giving skilled direction through the jungle.

One day as the party was moving along, the American hunters noticed that their native burden-bearers were not in sight. The leader of the party retraced his steps along the path that had been cut through the brush to find the natives lying in the grass at the side of the path and resting. Much perturbed, the white man inquired, "What is the meaning of this?" After all, they were hired to do a job. Why were they not doing it? The reply of the leader was this: "We had to stop long enough to let our souls catch up to our bodies."

Yes, we need this experience, too, in the whirling, busy world in which we live. You and I are living in an age of speed, the speed of transportation and of communication, the competition in the business world, and of being thrown into the world's melting pots—socially and economically—whether our minds and spirits are readied or not for the rubbing of elbows with our neighbors. And with this age of speed come great demands of pressure which so often result in a lapse that exists between the rush and movement of our physical selves and the abilities of our souls—our moral and our spiritual selves—to keep up with the rush of the day.

General Jumbo Wilson, during the Second World War, was to be responsible for the evacuation of Crete. He and his party made their way from the base down to the shore where they were to be picked up by a destroyer. When they arrived at the jetty the destroyer had not yet come. His aides were very much disturbed. They asked him what he was going to do. His reply was, "I'll do what many other soldiers have done. I'll sit on my baggage and wait!"

Samuel, the prophet, gave such advice to King Saul. Samuel had been given the responsibility of locating Saul that he might anoint Saul as king of Israel. They met as Saul, together with his party, was moving out of a little village. Samuel said to Saul, "Stand thou still awhile, that I may show thee the Word of God." Saul, sit on your baggage awhile that you may hear what the Lord has to say to you.

"Stand thou still awhile." Perhaps this sounds like heresy amidst the unconscious but prideful philosophy of an age caught up in an idolatrous worship of unrelenting drive and ambition. But whether heresy or not to the American mind, this is the wisdom of God: "Stand thou still awhile. Stop in the busy rush of life. Sit on your baggage and wait!" In the experience of doing this, you and I can learn some things of immeasurable importance. We can find not only physical and mental strength but spiritual and moral strength as well.

More Than Things

I FIND MYSELF disturbed when I look over that masterful work that was completed by Gibbon in the year 1787 entitled *The Decline and Fall of the Roman Empire.* Let me list for you five reasons that he gives for the fall of that empire. First, the rapid increase of divorce—the undermining of the dignity and sanctity of the home, which is the basis of human society. Second, higher and higher taxes and the spending of public monies for free bread and circuses for the populace. Third, the mad craze for pleasure—some sports becoming every year more exciting and more brutal. Fourth, the building of gigantic armaments when the real enemy was within the decadence of the people. Fifth, the decay of religion—faith fading into mere form, losing touch with life and becoming impotent to guide the people.

I cannot look at a picture such as this which comes from years gone by without taking a look at our today, for you and I find ourselves involved in a type of setting that reflects some of these same things. Charles Malik, the United Nations representative from the government of Lebanon, had this to say when he was asked just what was his opinion of the Americans: "Well, if I hadn't seen the Christians and didn't know first-hand about American Christianity; if I had to judge you only from your diplomats and your soldiers, only from your businessmen and your tourists, only from your newspapers and your radio and your motion pictures, I would probably be more impressed by Russia."

Now this is a startling statement which you and I find

31

difficult to absorb. What he was trying to get at was this—that we in America are sometimes trying to compete with Communism and with Russia on exactly the same level. We are claiming that democracy will give people a higher standard of living. "If the Russians say we will give every man a house, then you in the democracy say, 'We'll give him a mansion,'" said Malik. "If the Russians say Communism will give every man an automobile, you say 'That's nothing. Democracy will give him two automobiles.' And if the Russians say Communism will give a man a radio, you retort 'Democracy will give him a television set.'" Malik concluded that "you're just trying to outbid Russia on the level of gross materialism when you have something far more important to give to the world, and that is the spiritual ideals of a Christian America. Give these and you can compete, for the hearts of men are looking for more than things—they're looking for that which is real on the inside."

More than things! No individual finds satisfaction merely in things. Things—beautiful, ingenious, labor-saving—certainly have their place. The Almighty God has made their existence possible. But the realm of the soul cannot experience fulfillment alone in that which is physical. For the soul "longs, yea faints for the courts of the Lord." "For a man's life does not consist in the abundance of his possessions." Human personality, therefore, cannot know completeness if it be sterile in spirit.

Jesus Christ said by way of fulfilling this—man's deepest need—"I am come that they may have life, and have it abundantly." Old Testament scripture records, "Not by might, nor by power, but by my spirit, says the Lord of hosts."

The decline and fall of the spirit can become God's "rise and shine."

Unsung Heroes

THE OFTEN unnamed and unsung heroes of the world are among the fine women of the world. Not the least of these are the mothers. Who can measure their influence on the lives of their children and others as well?

The King of Persia, Darius, once announced that great honor and power would be given to the young man who wrote a sentence about the greatest power which in the judgment of the court would be deemed to be the wisest and most correct answer. The sentences were written, sealed, and placed under the king's pillow. In the morning, court was assembled and each young man was called before it to read and to defend his statement.

The first had written, "Wine is the strongest." He told how it could level all rank, make a pauper think he was a prince, make men forget their pain and sorrow, make them forget their honor, awakening in them a hidden person of evil and causing them to commit acts which later they cannot recollect having done.

The second had written, "The king is strongest." He explained that the king was only a man, yet his power was unlimited. At his command armies marched out to battle. Farmers and vineyard owners paid taxes to him. His word was law.

The third had written, "Woman is the strongest. Kings might be great and powerful but none exist but what is born of a woman. Without a woman, men cannot be. For the sake of a woman, men will give up gold, silver, their power, their country, their godly life; and there are examples for each of these. For the sake of a woman, men will cross seas, jungles, and rivers; will fight beasts and even kill other men. What could be stronger than woman?" the third asked. He was declared the winner.

How remarkable a story has been written in the history of time by the influence of women! Dr. Elton Trueblood, the eminent Quaker philosopher, once said of the women of the Bible, "Watch for the phrase in the books of Kings and Chronicles, 'And his mother was.' " This, he emphasized, was usually followed by the phrase, "And he did what was *right* in the sight of the Lord" or "And he did what was *evil* in the sight of the Lord." In placing the name of a king's mother and the evaluation of his reign side by side the Hebrews showed how powerful they regarded the role of a mother to be.

Dr. McClaren, a great preacher, told of visiting with a Scotch mother. She was a discouraged little woman. She felt that as a child of God she had made little contribution to the world—that she had been a failure. Dr. McClaren asked her about her children and she told him this story. She said that her son Matthew was a minister, that her son Mark was a Christian doctor, that her son Luke was a Christian business-man and that her son John was a Christian father. This, in effect, was Dr. McClaren's answer: "You have been no fail-ure. You may have felt like it because you were so busy with dishes, housework and all the rest as you brought up your family. But all the time you had an unseen partner who was working through your life and through the Word in the hearts of these sons so that they became the Christian characters and personalities that they are." Dr. McClaren concluded, "You know, mother, I'd like to live in your mansion in glory."

The Apostle Paul once wrote to Timothy, "I am reminded of your sincere faith, a faith that dwelt first in your grandmother Lois and in your mother Eunice and now, I am sure, dwells in you."

While Alexander the Great entertained the kings and nobles of the court of Persia, he appeared wearing only the clothes which had been woven for him by his mother, Olympia, who was the daughter of a chieftain, the wife of the king, the mother of a conqueror. There is a direct relationship between what we carry around today and what others have given to us before. Long ago, you and I discarded the clothes that were made for us by the loving hands of our mothers and yet, in a certain sense, when it comes to life and character, we are still wearing what our mothers wove into our lives a long time ago.

You Count

A SPORTS editor recently pointed up something rather thought-provoking in his column when he reminded his readers that an athletic team is made up of more than stars. Every one on the team counts. Though there may be one football player who scores most of the touchdowns, he does not cross that goal line often without the quarterback having called the right signals, the halfbacks having feinted and blocked and the linemen having opened the hole in the opposing line. From Halsey Hall, from Bernie Bierman, from your favorite sportscaster, you have heard this same emphasis: every man counts.

Now, it is not always true that every individual feels that way, whether it be in sports, on the job, or in any field of human relationships. You may have read in the newspaper of a machinist in Milwaukee who was arrested for his own kind of sabotage in the shop. Being too lazy, or thinking the way he handled his job to be quite unimportant, he had allowed the steel shavings to go back into the machine rather than to wheel them out of the shop in a wheelbarrow. The machine was wrecked. The damage he had done turned out to be of immeasurable importance. Here was a man who counted —negatively.

Sometimes we count positively only by our willingness to sublimate our "solo" talents for the greater effectiveness of the group. The *Messiah,* sung every year in the city of Minneapolis, involves a 1,200-voice choir. Whenever I listen to a mass choir like that I am reminded of a little incident that

I heard and saw years ago when the late Dr. F. Melius Christiansen, the famed director of the St. Olaf choir, was leading a mass choral group. Suddenly he stopped the entire group and said, "There's a voice that is sticking out over there in the soprano section. I want a straight voice from Shingle Creek." This was no place for solo histrionics. If this soprano were to count positively, then here was a place for her to blend her voice with others in order to produce the rich and massive effects that would bring inspiration to the audience.

Whether you like it or not, you count at this moment as a plus or a minus, whatever your role may be. Every single one of us counts! The guard and the tackles and the ends as well as the break-away runner on a football team; the man in the shop as well as the man at the executive desk in the company office; the blending voices in a mass choir as well as the solo voice in concert. Every single one of us is important!

It is interesting, I think, that Jesus never met an unimportant person. He always dealt with the individual. He had high regard for human personality. Some of those with whom he spent the most time and in whom He indicated a special interest were the so-called "little people." Jesus knew their real value, not alone in God's sight, but also to the world around them. They were the "stuff" of which a better world would be made, for they were the faithful children of God at work in the world of man.

Jesus said so in the highest compliment He could pay. He said—"You are the salt of the earth . . You are the light of the world."

Is Your World Too Small?

HAVE YOU heard the story about the Hungarian refugee whose wife and children turned their backs on him to walk back into Hungary, and away from the freedom that he had found for himself and also for them? As I read about it and realized how his world must have collapsed for him, I recalled a little incident that took place recently.

She was just a little bit of a woman that we met. In fact, we didn't really meet her. We only encountered her for brief seconds, passing through a doorway. My wife, three of our daughters and I were entering a hotel dining room. As we went in the door, this little lady was coming out. With a quick glance at our girls, she looked up at us and said smilingly, "I see that you have your world with you. I had two sons and they were my little world."

"I see that you have your world with you." What an intriguing statement! How very descriptive! As parents, we do have a wonderful little world in our families. I suspect that we will never quite get over the wonder of it. That is as it should be. Other folks, perhaps not privileged to be parents, also have their meaningful little world. It may be the little world of some particularly worthwhile friendship. It may be the little world of their work, or if not a vocation, some avocation.

But sometimes that most immediate little world takes a harsh blow and collapses. If that world is too small, or too

circumscribed, some folks have real difficulty when life
leaves what to them only may seem "second best." What
different reactions there are! Lord Byron and Scott both had
club feet. You sit down to read what Byron wrote and you
sense in his poems some of the bitterness and the cynicism of
his heart. Then you turn to what Scott wrote. Immediately
you catch some of the radiance that he knew and passed on
with a strengthening force to those who read his writings.

Or think of Beethoven whose ears could not hear but
his soul could, and so his heart could sing. From his silent
world he composed some of the most wonderful music that
ever has come to man. Or, think of Helen Keller, blind, deaf,
and dumb; yet, who, walking in her flower garden, could
stoop and pick a flower, smell it and say, "It's beautiful!"

Or recall the frequent bitterness of old age. Then com-
pare it with a Grandma Moses as an artist, or of a Victor
Hugo, writing his best compositions, not before he was sixty
or seventy-five, but when he was between eighty-five and
ninety-five years old. It was then he wrote: "I haven't written the best within me and I look forward to Eternity in which
I can finish my great work."

I think, too, of Paul, with his faith in God as the core of
his world. He once said, "I can do all things through Christ
who strengthens me;" and once again, "I have learned in
whatsoever state I am, therewith to be content."

This is not a mere resignation to a status quo, nor mere
acquiescence. But it is allowing God into your world and it
is letting Him give to you a measure of the leaven which will
widen your world, and deepen your world, and heighten your
world. Whatever life may bring you can in the end provide its
own leaven, and further enrich and deepen and widen life
for you.

The Length of Your Nose

HOW IMPORTANT is your appearance? Have you ever wondered?

This is the story that came out of London on this subject. Mrs. Terry Phillips—so says the press—won a prize on a TV show. Her prize was the money to get a new nose.

Mrs. Phillips is forty years old and supposedly has one of the longest noses this side of Jimmy Durante. When she talked about it she said, "I get chilblains on it in the winter and I scald it when I take a hot drink." This hard-luck story gained the most sympathy when it was told on a TV show, and Mrs. Phillips' award was the prize of a hundred pounds —about $280—to reshape her nose.

Meanwhile Mrs. Phillips' small daughter, Shirley, had something to say about it. She cried bitterly when she heard that mother was going to have some changes made on her nose. She pleaded, "Mother, don't have your nose cut off. I like you the way you are." Mrs. Phillips' husband agreed. The money is now going to four charitable organizations in her home town instead.

How important *are* the looks with which we have been endowed—the looks we carry around on the outside? Oh, it is true that they make some difference. Abraham Lincoln once suggested that we do have a great deal to do with what we look like on the outside because this reflects what we are like on the inside. Smiles or grouchy frowns tell a good deal about us. But whether we are handsome, or not so handsome, beautiful or not so beautiful, this is not as important as we may have thought it to be. What is truly important is what we are on the inside. Real beauty or ugliness is actually not a matter of facial features but of what we are in our spirits and personalities. This flows out of one's heart.

The prophet Samuel on one occasion had an experience that taught him a lesson along these same lines. He had been given the responsibility of selecting and anointing a new king over Israel. He was to be guided by God in making the choice. The Old Testament record gives us this story. "When they (the sons of Jesse) came, he (Samuel) looked on Eliab and thought, 'Surely the Lord's anointed is before him.' But the Lord said to Samuel, 'Do not look on his appearance or on the height of his stature, because I have rejected him; for the Lord sees not as man sees; man looks on the outward appearance, but the Lord looks on the heart.' "

I doubt that what the Lord said to Samuel was anything brand new to him. Perhaps it was no more new than it is to you or to me. But we can use some reminding sometimes, and reminded of this truth, do some reappraising of our too often superficial appraisals of others. Real quality, we now discover, lies on occasion in some surprisingly uninteresting or even crude appearing human packages. When we need more than someone merely capable of dressing up the place, we make our choices and call for our help from among those whose hearts are right, real people all the way from the inside out. Far more important than the length of a nose is the depth of a heart.

We, Too, Are People

IT IS YOUR LIFE and here in America most of us realize
how good a life it is. For one thing we know or can know
that we count! News stories tell us of the incident in Hungary where a whole train-load of a thousand rebels were
rescued by their own Nationalist friends near the city of
Budapest, saved from being carried into Russia or Siberia
where they would have been reduced to slave laborers.

Yugoslavian officials, in another news account, record
how their nation and people in their political thinking are
split in two; there are the Stalinists, and there are those who
want the freedom to live under a democracy.

Down in Buenos Aires a woman hung by her fingers
from the edge of a balcony at the Embassy of Communist
Roumania. Though she was a Roumanian, she did not want
to return to her Communist-held homeland. She was seeking escape and freedom for herself and for her child. Because that child had been born in Argentina, she was finally
given asylum in that country.

People in vast areas of the world are crying out, "We,
too, are people!" This is a voice that is being heard from
large masses in India. A Pakistani says, "No longer will
we be treated with contempt either because of our ideology
or otherwise." Thus there is an awakening awareness in
people everywhere that they count, or that they want to count.

Some time ago I came out of Los Angeles by plane and
was flying across the deserts of Nevada, and then over the

Colorado Rockies toward Denver. As I looked out of the plane window late at night, I saw the blinking lights of a little village down on the desert, then the isolated lights of little mountain cabins. As I saw them, I thought how seemingly unimportant these little spots were, known to very few people in all of America and less than this to the world beyond. The individuals and peoples represented by these lights had perhaps a few relatives and friends scattered here and there who knew of them and were concerned, but for the most part one could imagine that these scattered glows of life could count but little in the greater lights of the world's masses huddled together throughout the globe.

Then we came to the city of Denver where there were the greater myriads of lights representing many thousands of people, some in crowded areas, others spilling outward into the more sparsely populated residential and suburban areas. There, I thought, are so many lights—so many lives. How can one against so many count in the ebb or flow of life toward eternity? I was reminded of some words out of Psalm 8 that read, "What is man that thou are mindful of him, and the son of man, that thou dost care for him?" These are people and each one counts. All of them count. And from the psalm these words, "Yet thou hast made him little less than God, and dost crown him with glory and honor" (RSV).

Every man is a created being, created by the Almighty God. When we have that realization for ourselves, as well as for others, it changes our whole attitude toward self and others.

There are great numbers of people who feel that they do not count. Defeatism is spelled out by every word they speak. Frustration and despair or simple meaninglessness in life are part of every day's diet. They sit in the doctor's office, in the pastor's office, in the psychologist's or the psychiatrist's office and they say by their manner or in speech, "I don't count." But they do. They do because they are God's created beings. We are not only children of the world but we can be, in Christ, citizens of heaven— yes, fortunate enough to be citizens in a great democracy but, more than that, the very children of God.

This makes all the difference. Life lived alone and unrelated to Christ is like fish-life lived apart from water or bird-life lived apart from air. Only the atmosphere of Christ's redeeming love surrounding human life can make life what God intended it to be—"crowned with glory and honor."

From Rejected to Resurrected

YOU HAVE come to the close of another day. I suspect that, like most folks, you have been thinking over the incidents of the day, recounting what has gone onto this day's page. No doubt there have been satisfactions; perhaps for some of you disappointments and regrets as well. But it is a remarkable world in which we live, is it not? It is remarkable because of the new opportunities that are given in spite of failures that may have existed in the past or, if not failures, some limitations that may have been quite beyond control.

The other day I chatted with two German refugees who have just recently arrived in America. How they stand in awe and wonder at this American nation of ours and all the opportunities that lie before the people here! The husband, who had spent three and a half years in a prison camp in Russia, has now the thrill of brand new opportunties before him.

This is true in so many different aspects of life. Defeat, misfortune and failure enter into the lives of most people at one time or another. The question really is—what is it that can grow out of defeat? What can come out of misfortune or failure?

A marble block, spoiled in the quarry, was thrown away. There was a tiny fissure and so it had been cast aside. That was, however, before Michelangelo came wandering along. His keen eye detected the beauty of the rejected stone. He began to chip it, a little here and some there, and more and more of its beauty became revealed. One day a heroic "David" emerged from the rejected stone—a marble figure to amaze the world. The scrap rejected by other men had been glorified now forever.

How often the observing eye sees a thing of surprising beauty and usefulness made from the scraps another has tossed aside—a picture framed in a square of shells; bit of glass artistically arranged in a putty background; a little home, cozy and attractive, with love at the center of it but with nothing to suggest the used lumber that went into its walls—boards from the sides of condemned railway cars . . . again, from the junkpile of the rejected a framework of happiness.

Deaf, blind and dumb, surely it seemed Helen Keller would be cast aside to a dull and dreary existence for all of her days. But with indomitable courage and patience, and aided by an equally indomitable Miss Sullivan, her devoted teacher and companion, she took life's rejected outlook and from it carved a life of angelic beauty.

Or an awkward, unprepossessing lad in a wilderness of poverty and privation—what chance for him? I wondered about that as I stood down there in Salem, Illinois . . . yes, wondered if there were any chance at all. And I suppose he wondered, too, as he faced what seemed a tragic, hopeless lack of knowledge. In his cabin home until late in the night he solved his problems, not with paper and pencil, but with scraps of charcoal picked from the big fireplace and with the back of a shovel that was used for a slate. No wonder he went to the White House to share a place forever on a pedestal beside his nation's George Washington. Surely Abraham Lincoln took a fate that seemed all scraps and ruin to fashion a noble life of honor and of service.

Out of a pile of scrap iron, one makes a useful household utensil. Out of a block of wood from a pile at a kitchen door, another fashions a sweet-toned violin.

So it is in life—with things. But not only things; for it has to do with people, and with people's hearts as well. And God in Jesus Christ has given the greatest opportunity of all to take the scraps from out of the past and from this past to re-fashion and remold a new and wonderful life. For it was this Christ who redeemed man, who made it possible for him to become a new creature, to give him a new life with which to face the new tomorrows. "Therefore, if any one is in Christ, he is a new creation; the old has passed away, behold, the new has come."

Plus Ultra

THERE IS A grocery store in our city that has an unusual sign over its front windows. It reads: "Ne plus ultra." I am sure that few who read that sign know its meaning. Perhaps fewer still are aware that this was once the motto on the coat of arms for the nation of Spain. This was before Columbus discovered the new world and the words in Latin meant: "There is *nothing* beyond." All that the people in pre-Columbus days really understood was the three-mile limit off shore. They suspected that beyond that the world was an indefinable void that dropped off into space not too far away.

But Columbus set sail to discover that there was something beyond—a whole new world. When he returned to tell that story to his nation and people, they changed the motto from "Ne plus ultra" to "Plus ultra." There is *more* beyond. That is, there is a world beyond—a great, fabulous, wonderful world that they had never known before.

Every day we are making similar discoveries. I can recall years ago watching the famous flyer, "Speed" Holman, at Wold Chamberlain Field when he piloted his aeroplane in a 300 mph. power dive. To all of the spectators this was a fantastic feat. Today—thirty years later—three B-52 Stratofortresses have circled the entire globe in about 45 hours at an average of more than 500 miles per hour on the straightaway.

There are other areas, too, where we recognize that there is always more beyond. The businessman discovers it in his business world, the football team in its athletic program, the

48

editor at his desk in developing a new pattern of communication. It is true in science, in the laboratory, in advertising, in one area after another. The medical world discovers an almost sure method of sex determination before birth. The scientific world startles us with an even more amazing performance with its electronic brains.

It is necessary, however, that our new discoveries shall be not only in the realms which I have mentioned but in the moral and spiritual world as well. The poet Edwin Markham was once persuaded by some of his friends to put the savings of a lifetime into a precarious investment. The day came when he was informed that he had lost everything he had. At first he strongly resented this loss, but not for long. His fundamental Christian attitude asserted itself. He took a sheet of paper and idly drew two circles. Almost before he knew it, he had written his now famous quatrain, "Outwitted":

> "He drew a circle that shut me out—
> Heretic, rebel, a thing to flout;
> But love and I had the wit to win—
> We drew a circle and took him in."

The world of the impossibles is constantly becoming the the world of the possibles in our remarkable age. It is high time that we rediscover the spiritual powers that change impossibles in moral and spiritual realms. The resources have been available all the time. We have only failed to claim and use them under God in Christ. Here hatred turns to love, bitterness turns to forgiveness and friendship, defeat turns to victory.

This is the way of Jesus Christ. This is Plus Ultra. "No eye has seen, nor ear heard, nor the heart of man conceived, what God has prepared for those who love him."

Dreams Walking

To DAY-DREAM is one thing, to have vision is quite another. Day-dreaming can cause some people to live so much in the future that the present is left without any meaning.

"Did you ever see a dream walking? Well, I did!" You may remember this popular song number of several years ago. We can be like dreams walking, can we not? The writer of that particular hit tune had reference, of course, to some beautiful young lady who was like a walking dream; that can be very lovely. But we may be dreams walking without being one whit beautiful or handsome. This may be in a good sense or one not so good—it all depends. If we are simply day-dreamers walking, then the chances are that we rarely buckle down to the realities of life to deal with them as we must. But there can be a "plus" side to dreaming. This "plus" side is what we might better call vision, and vision is important.

Few individuals, organizations, churches, companies, communities or nations really go anywhere without vision. Now this is far more than mere day-dreaming. It is creative dreaming tied to some action, some effort.

Some of you may remember Grandpa's old musket. That musket was loaded a bit differently than the modern rifle. Grandpa would pour powder into the barrel, wad it down and then put shot in after it. But one day Grandpa made a mistake. He put the shot in first, then the powder, so that when he took a bead on the target and pulled the trigger, all he got for his efforts was an empty click.

Dreaming without effort is like that. All you get is an empty click! The Apostle Paul was one who had vision, then tied it up to action. He had a clear-cut vision of who Jesus Christ was, the Saviour of the world and his Saviour. This was vision as important as a man can get. Where he had been spiritually blind, now he could see. And he saw more than just within the sphere of his own little self. What he had found he knew the world needed, most particularly Europe as far as his responsibility was concerned; and he took his new-found faith there to give it away to others, the first man in history to do so! His dream, his vision, moved into action. Under God, he wrote one of the greatest chapters in the history of the Christian church.

A dream walking! We need to be more than that. We need to be men and women of great dreams, great vision in action! It is then that the Christian church on earth is built, that communities know and achieve high purposes, that homes are strengthened and enriched. It is then that this world of ours becomes God's world!

"Wherefore . . . I was not disobedient to the heavenly vision."

To Change a World

TWO TOTALLY contrasting elements are at work in the world seeking somehow to achieve what would seem to be an equivalent result. One of these is love. The other is force. In international relationships, force is usually used to dissuade enemy nations from taking any action that would bring about war. But there is also the element of love when human society seeks through creative friendships to alleviate the tensions that exist. Now which of these is the better?

The Magazine Digest some years ago told an engaging little story of love as the transforming force in human relationships. A high school girl in the Cincinnati Union Station crossed the waiting room to a mother who was seated with her two very fussy little children waiting for a train. To the mother she said, "Why don't you let me take care of your babies for a little while? You go get something to eat and get a little rest." The mother did just that. She was gone for an hour and came back remarkably refreshed. Her train was called and she left with her little ones.

But for the high school girl this was not all. She had spied another mother busy with her little children. She, too, was tired and worn from traveling. Again the young girl said, "Can I help you?" One traveler who had been watching all this spoke to the girl and asked, "What is it that you are doing?" The girl replied, "You know, I live with an aunt right across the street from the station and every day after high school is out I come over here to the station for a couple of hours. You see, during the war my mommy and

I and a couple of our sisters and brothers had to travel a good deal all over the country when our father was in the army, and mother got so terribly tired. Mother often said to me that somehow or another I had just the knack of taking care of little children. Now when school is out I come over here every day for an hour or two and I always find a mother who's all tired and worn and I tell her, 'Why don't you go away for a little while and I'll take care of your little children?' You see, my mother died and I think it's one of the best things I can do to show how much my mother meant to me in giving this love to some other mother."

Love carries a tremendous amount of weight. Sometimes we may feel that we do not make a very big dent in this world of ours, that the things that we do are rather insignificant. Yet each of us, if we live in the spirit of Jesus Christ, can love. And when this force of love is applied on the level of every-day relationships among two or three or more who knows what widening ripples it can effect, until whole communities can be changed! All because someone cared enough —loved enough!

"How precious is thy steadfast love, O God!
The children of men take refuge in the shadow of thy
    wings.
. . . for with thee is the fountain of life;
in thy light do we see light." (Psalm 36:7,9)

Faith in Action

ONE OF THE things that this beloved nation of ours always needs is a people who do not apologize for their faith.

John Carroll, a United Press sportswriter, brings us this interesting story out of Pittsburgh and the sports world. Dale Dodrill, who specializes in knocking down runners during the professional football season for the Pittsburgh Steelers, is busy during the winter season helping people back on their religious underpinnings. The five-time all-pro middle guard is actively engaged as a layman missionary for his church when it conducts its annual nationwide drive to put religion back into every home. During the football season it is pretty tough for a professional player to get to church services as often as he desires. "When the season ends, I try to do as much as I can to help out," Dodrill said.

To "help out," Dodrill visited homes in his suburban Pittsburgh neighborhood "running interference" for those who have strayed away from the church and who now want to return. "All I do is talk to the folks and try to interest them in the church, sort of get them back to Christ," he said. "If they agree, I go with them to services and meetings. It's like running interference so they don't have to go back in the game cold. After all, in most cases where a home is not in order, you'll find there is no religion," he said. "Without faith there is not much base for a stable, happy home life."

"The former Colorado A & M athlete explained his feelings in quiet, sincere tones," wrote Carroll, "which presented a marked contrast to the hustle he displays on the gridiron where he is rated by his coaches as pound for pound probably the best lineman in football."

Now a six-year veteran of the national football league and shooting for seven, Dale admits that he calls on prayer not only in everyday life but also before, during and after each game. "Before we take the field for a game our coach, Walt Geisling," he told, "sets aside time so that the players can offer up their own prayers. It may surprise you but just about every Steeler makes the most of that time."

"Do you have any special little prayer that you offer up before swinging into action against the best football talent in the world?" he was asked by Carroll. "No, but what usually comes out is a prayer not to win or lose. I usually ask God to spare the players on both sides any serious injuries," Dodrill said.

Here is a man who makes no apology for his Christian faith. He is not alone. I have known and seen the same creative faith in other top athletes, professionals and amateurs. There are few with as great an opportunity to be convincing examples for America's youngsters, and they know it.

Faith exemplified in action is not limited in possibility to the world of sports. A dynamic, healthy Christianity can be seen in thousands of men from common laborers to top-flight executives. They are the men who, like the heroic Apostle Paul, are able to say in word and action, ". . . I am not ashamed of the Gospel: it is the power of God for salvation to everyone who has faith."

Taking Your Picture

A MIDDLE-AGED self-respecting wife and mother became disgusted with her husband for his drunken orgies. Late one night he returned home in this familiar drunken stupor, slumped into a kitchen corner, clothes torn, hair matted, face bruised, and promptly went to sleep.

His wife hurried across the street. "Bring your camera over to my house," she asked of her neighbor, a skilled photographer. "At this hour?" "Yes, please—as a favor." The wife had her neighbor focus his camera on the huddled mass in the kitchen corner. She asked him to say nothing of this but to develop the picture as soon as possible.

A couple of mornings later the husband awoke to find two pictures on the bedroom dresser: one a graphic photo of a disheveled and dissipated tramp slumped in the kitchen corner but beside that a very handsome portrait of the young man on his wedding day twenty years earlier. The shocking contrast in these two portraits gave this man the determination to become a changed individual in his home and a credit to his community as well.

Sometimes we may take a good look at ourselves and rather like what we see. But I am sure there are many times when you and I are not in the least happy about what we see in ourselves. It may come as quite a shock to catch an honest picture of what we are like at any given moment. This is true whether we think of ourselves individually or collectively. There are times when we read our newspapers, listen to the newscasts, and catch a picture of an entire segment of society that does not present a pleasant profile.

I am sure that all of us were disappointed in the Montgomery, Alabama, story when mixed recreation from billiards to baseball was very recently officially banned in that community.

I was in Montgomery not too long ago. It looked much like many another American city. We drove its wide downtown streets. The Capitol building is beautifully located at the head of a broad loop avenue sloping uphill. Across from the front doors of the Capitol building stands the neat, medium-sized, red brick Baptist church served by Dr. Martin Luther King, a name made familiar these past months in the race struggle in Alabama. This red brick church was the startling reminder that in our free America part of us is not really free at all.

White and colored cannot play together? Yes, that is the story. It is a story that seems incredible at this juncture after watching some of our baseball teams in action—the Brooklyn Dodgers, the Milwaukee Braves, and others with a Jackie Robinson, a Henry Aaron, a Willie Mays—by now a long, long list of young men of another race, key men on their respective teams.

Perhaps it is that now our state basketball tournament with all its thrills and display of sportsmanship simply sets off a Montgomery incident in greater relief. Not that differently located on the map of our land we, too, might not be involved with the same blindness. But the thrill of the tournaments in our state, the bigness of spirit found in the players, whether they come from a school of 47 pupils or from a school of 2,000, teaches us something of sportsmanship applicable in many and varied walks of life.

It was back in my own high school basketball days that my parents placed a meaningful plaque on the wall of my room. The verse inscribed on it is a familiar one by Edgar A. Guest:

> "We can't all play a winning game—
> Someone is sure to lose.
> But we can play so that our name
> No one may dare accuse.
> And when the Master Referee
> Scores against our name,
> It won't be if we've won or lost
> But how we've played the game."

The Snare of Preparation

THERE IS A great deal of day-dreaming in the makeup of most of us, some of it good, some of it not good. There is some day-dreaming from which we ought to be awakened. I am thinking now of the type which we may brand as a "green pasture" illusion—that the grass is always greener on the other side of the fence. The psychologist, William Marston, one time asked 2,999 people, "What are you living for?" He was startled to find in the tone of their answers that there was an unbelievable number who were simply enduring the present while they waited for a better future. Actors and entertainers doing bit parts were waiting for the "big chance." People in business were thinking of their present job as an unnecessary and undeserved interlude, a mere marking of time until fate opened a door to something better.

One middle-aged mother said, "I only hope that my nerves can stand the ordeal until my husband retires and the children get homes of their own. I'm living for that blessed day when I can get a little rest."

Tolstoy perhaps had a better phrase for this pattern of life and thought. He called it the "snare of preparation," the fallacy of habitually thinking of today as a mere preparation for tomorrow, thinking of the present situation as a sort of drab waiting room in a bus station where we must sit and wait until the bus comes and takes us to a better place. Even the bus trip is a marking of time, something we have to endure until we arrive. When we do arrive, there is

always a greener pasture further on and life for many becomes a series of waiting rooms.

I like the imaginative thought of the writer who was walking very rapidly down a country road one day, his mind full
of anxious thoughts, when he seemed to hear a slow drolling
voice come up from the road itself, asking "Why don't you
saunter along? Why don't you take it a little easier? Maybe
you think there is nothing worthwhile on the road but the
end of it? Believe me, there is something more. If you do
not find love, and joy, and goodness on the road, they will
not be waiting for you at the end."

We stand looking out into life, into our family situations,
our work, our community of which we are a part. There
are whole companies of thoughts that can make our faces
drawn, our spirits heavy. But perhaps we ought to catch that
something of which Jacob suddenly became aware a long
time ago when he said, "Surely the Lord is in his place;
and I did not know it."

"Surely the Lord is in *this* place . . ." How often we
treat the present as though the Lord and His goodness lay
only in the future and elsewhere. Yet, scores of people over
the years have indicated that it has been in the hard hours
of life that they have found God and have begun to learn
how to live.

For the child of God the end of the road will mean eternal
life. But there is a sense in which that life eternal begins at
the moment of faith. Because this is true, life is worth living
now for "surely the Lord is in *this* place."

An Antidote For Fear

ONE AFTERNOON each week the social worker of our congregation and I are in conference over some of our perplexed people with critical needs. Recently with one of our women we discovered a paralyzing fear that was undermining all of life for her.

Fear is something shared by a great number of people in the world. Here is a little story quoted from the Boston Globe that may point up an answer to it:

It was on an Easter morning in the year 1799. The armies of Napoleon were moving over the continent of Europe conquering all that came in their way. The sun shone down brightly on Feldkirk, a little town on the river immediately within the border of Austria. Quite early on that morning there suddenly appeared on the heights above the town the glittering weapons of 18,000 French soldiers under the command of General Messina. Quickly the town council met and decided to send a group to Messina with the keys to the town and a petition for mercy. It was in the midst of all this fear and confusion that the old dean of the church stood up, serene, and with no thought of fear. "It is Easter day," he said. "We have been reckoning on our own strength and it is but weakness. Let us ring the bells and have our service as usual. We will leave our troubles in the hands of the Higher Power."

Soon from all the church spires of Feldkirk bells rang out joyfully. The streets became thronged with worshippers on their way to church. Louder and more triumphant pealed the bells, ringing out the glad news of the living Christ.

The French army heard the sounds of rejoicing, and Messina concluded that there could be but one reason for it: that the Austrian army had approached during the night. Messina ordered his men to break camp and almost before the bells had ceased their ringing, long before the Easter services were over, the French army was in retreat. Not a tent, not a soldier, nor a glittering bayonet was to be seen on the heights above Feldkirk. Fear found its defeat at the hands of the Higher Power.

But fear is shared by millions throughout the world, whatever their position or station in life may be. A sultan of Turkey spent $900 of his millions each night to have his bedroom guarded. Hitler, who ruled with a tremendous sweep of power, would have no visitors if they were not first searched for weapons. A university professor lived for many years with such fear in his heart and such superstition in his mind that he never went beyond the certain small area between his home and his classroom. In the same city lived the man who wrote the humorous counterpart of Carnegie's "How to Win Friends and Influence People" entitled "How to Lose Friends and Alienate People" but found life to be not worth living. In our professedly Christian America an estimated 125 million dollars a year goes to fortune tellers of various kinds with the hope of outguessing tomorrow and its fears. But the fears go on and the prediction business continues at a brisk pace.

Long ago a Psalmist said, "I lift up my eyes to the hills. From whence does my help come? My help comes from the Lord who made heaven and earth." Here, friend, is the real answer to fear. The Almighty is more substantial than the rock He formed. Hs is more gentle than the soft wind of summer. He has more tender concern than the bird for her young. He cares for His own. When they lean trustingly on Him, they find that He more than adequately meets their needs.

Perhaps fear is really a sense of "aloneness" in a setting of fragile supports; courage, a sense of "oneness" in a setting of adequate supports. What then is Christian courage but a quality of life which grows out of a "oneness" with God in Christ set in the framework of His promise— "my grace is sufficient for you"?

Eleven Hundred Wrong Ways

A MOUNTAIN CLIMBER, his guide by his side, stood erect to get a better view of the landscape that stretched out before him. His guide shouted to him, "On your knees, sir, on your knees. That is the only safe position for a man up here with this strong wind blowing."

As we look at the world about us, the millions of people everywhere carrying burdens too heavy for human strength, the only position a child of God *can* take is to be on his knees. Your approach and mine to our world of today with our needs and its needs should be that described in II Chronicles, "If my people who are called by my name humble themselves, and pray and seek my face, and turn from their wicked ways, then I will hear from heaven, and will forgive their sin and heal their land."

Humanity, it seems, is in somewhat of an experimental stage of trying not only how to live, but how *not* to live. Edison performed eleven hundred experiments in his search for a substance to use as a filament of an incandescent light. Eleven hundred failures. Someone then said to Edison, "You have wasted your time." "Oh, no," he answered, "I have found out eleven hundred ways not to proceed." Into as great despair as eleven hundred wrong ways may plunge a man, this need not be the end.

Two mountain climbers were lost in the Pyrenees mountains. They had to lie out all night and in the morning there was a tremendous snow storm. The wind roared, and trees and rocks tumbled down. One of the climbers was an old timer; the other was new to the sport. The newcomer shook with fear and said, "This is the end." "No," said the old timer, "don't be afraid. This is the way dawn comes in the Pyrenees mountains."

Ours is another rather dark hour in human history. We have tensions in international relationships. Human society within our own land has a case of nerves. But we still believe in the dawn. We believe that Jesus Christ and the church of Christ cannot fail. We believe that Christ can reign through the storm, through a world obsessed, through any convulsive upheaval. We believe that God can bring His dawn to our world—through eleven hundred wrong ways by One Right Way. "I am the way, and the truth, and the life; no one comes to the Father, but by me."

A Matter of Direction

TALL, BLOND, handsome Billy Graham, today's most popular spokesman for the Christian faith, literally took over New York's Madison Square Garden as a three-month setting for his pulpit and congregation. It was in that unusual place, more often packed with raucous fight crowds, that Graham had this to say: "Life can be sweet and sassy, like our modern cars, but if we have lost the key, we can't go any place. We have missed life somewhere then. Instead of our problems decreasing, they are multiplying. The simple truth is that we have lost contact with the Supernatural, with the Harmonizer and Co-ordinator of the universe. Like an aircraft in a storm which has lost contact with the control tower, we are circling, ever-circling, with our visibility zero. We can't touch our wheels to the ground."

Graham, concerned as he is about the spiritual and moral welfare of the people of New York City and of our entire beloved America, has as his real goal that which is found in an old word in the Christian vocabulary called "conversion." And what is conversion? Well, it has to do with a matter of an "about face" as a soldier puts it—a turning around from going the wrong direction to going the right direction.

Life is motion. It is a way. It is a walk. You, too, are going some place, becoming someone. Either you are moving upward or you are moving downward. It depends upon direction, upon which way you are facing.

And direction means everything. If you are facing the wrong direction, each step taken carries you farther from the man, the woman, you ought to become. Either you are becoming more—or you are becoming less. Either you are walking towards God—or away from Him.

A friend, Dick Halvorson of Washington, D. C., put it something like this: The difference between a Christian and a non-Christian is really a matter of 180-degrees. The Christian man faces Christ. The non-Christian has his back to Christ. Conversion is what takes place when the Spirit of God leads a man to an "about-face," a 180-degree turn. Visibility is now no longer zero. The aircraft of one's life has now made contact with "the control tower." A safe landing after a purposeful flight is assured. It is a matter of direction.

"All the ends of the earth shall remember and turn to the
     Lord;
and all the families of the nations shall worship before
     him.
For dominion belongs to the Lord, and he rules over the
     nations.
Yea, to him shall all the proud of the earth bow down;
before him shall bow all who go down to the dust, and
     he who cannot keep himself alive.
Posterity shall serve him;
men shall tell of the Lord to the coming generation,
and proclaim his deliverance to a people yet unborn,
     that he has wrought it."

The "Too Busyness" of Life

HOWARD WHITMAN, writing in "A Reporter in Search for God," recalls hearing of this epitaph on a tombstone. It read: "She died of things—He died providing them." Now obviously neither sex has a monopoly on being enslaved by *things*. All of us find ourselves being endangered in this area.

Henry David Thoreau said of the modern age that it is "enslaved by things material." We may have improved means but to unimproved ends. We have planes that get us there earlier, but we are not always sure what to do when we get there. We have high speed cars but, as one man has said, we also have "bigger fools knocking down bigger trees." We get news photos in a matter of seconds but what is pictured is not always worthwhile. We are mechanically capable of producing hundreds of times more than in the past but also we have a thousand more wants—some of them quite trivial. How easy it is to become involved in a "rat-race" with a goal of "more."

Some years ago a missionary by the name of Dan Crawford returned to England. He had been gone for twenty-five years without a return visit. As Crawford chatted with one of the Cabinet ministers, the Cabinet minister posed this thought: "I wish that I could borrow your eyes to see the changes that have taken place over the years." Crawford replied that he had discovered upon his return that the modern, materialistic young man had been robbed of his smile.

Robbed of his smile! This is possible in a world too involved in *things*.

One day I was visiting with a good friend of mine, Dr. Olaf Christiansen, the director of the St. Olaf Choir. Our conversation centered around the problems that arise when we are caught up in the "too-busyness of life." Dr. Christiansen told of a family ceremony that takes place annually at their summer cottage on the shores of Lake Michigan. Kept in the storehouse over the winter is the rudder of an old ship which once sailed the Great Lakes. Immediately upon the arrival of the family for the summer it is taken out to be hung in a conspicuous place. The purpose is this—to remind them to steer straight and to keep the right values in life.

We, too, need our reminders to "steer straight." All around us are influences and pressures that all too quickly push us off course. We find ourselves "majoring in minors" and by the same token, "minoring in majors." Human personality becomes subservient in value to profits, to personal successes—to *things*.

Holy Scripture reminds us of the same thing. Recall, if you will, that Christ Himself found it necessary to move away from the crowds and the press of life to a quiet place with the Father. The Psalmist on behalf of God reminded his reader, "Be still, and know that I am God." The New Testament records: "Do not lay up for yourselves treasures . . . where moth and rust consumes and where thieves break in and steal, but lay up for yourselves treasures in heaven."

These are rudders that steer life straight.

Give Yourself Away

TWO GUNMEN in St. Paul are being hunted for having unceremoniously taken away the sum of $3,000 from a supermarket. This is headline news. Such things always are.

But let me add something else to the news—yes, and to the headlines if headlines are to reflect the truly important. In total contrast to the St. Paul incident this does not have to do with taking away but rather with giving away.

David Dunn once wrote an arresting little book entitled "Try Giving Yourself Away." A copy came into my hands as a gift from a man who knew first hand what this meant. He was the late Walter Geist, president of the Allis Chalmers Corporation, a man who had been doing this all his life. Top executive over a World War II employment roll of 37,000 people, he never lost his human touch. It was no surprise to the "old timers" in the plant to see him move down an aisle between huge steel-cutting lathes checking and inspecting with a "Hi Bill, how's Mary?" or "Hello John, how's your ulcer?" Were you to call him on the phone, busy as he was, he would grasp one of four phones dangling from the corners of his desk to talk to you personally. When his church, the YMCA, the Community Chest or some little lady down the street needed his help, Walter was there—giving himself away. I am not at all sure that his early death did not result in part because of his constantly considering himself expendable in useful service to his fellow men.

Now someone may be tempted to say, "Yes, but I'm not a famous industrialist. My life can't mean very much to others." David Dunn upon hearing this would, I am sure, have replied with "Oh, can't it?" and would have answered with a simple illustration. "Suppose I am passing a neighborhood store in which I notice a particularly attractive window display. I say to myself, 'Someone put real thought into trimming that window, and he or she ought to know that at least one passerby appreciates it.' So I stop in, ask for the manager, and compliment him on the display. I find it always pleases a merchant to know that his windows are noticed, even though I may not buy a penny's worth of merchandise displayed in them. In one instance the clerk who trimmed the windows received a raise in pay as a result of my compliment." This is giving yourself away.

Jesus Christ highlighted this value a long time ago. You remember that He said, "Whosoever would save his life shall lose it; but whosoever will lose his life for my sake shall find it."

On occasion people speak of Christ as a wholly unrealistic visionary, a soft-touch dreamer. But what is more practical in terms of effective human relations than what Christ said and, by example, did? He was constantly "giving himself away" in life, and in death capped all examples of self-giving before or since.

What a different world this would be if all of us could learn that lesson. To live constantly with an awareness of others, to give ourselves away, leads us to the discovery that what others gain we gain too, for having expressed the spirit of the Master.

Try giving yourself away, will you? The world is waiting for people who will.

No Grist to Grind

HE STARTED your car, but you may not know his name. He gave you "power to pass" and perhaps saved your life. Yet his name may be strange to you. More recently, however, numerous articles have been telling the exciting story of Charles F. Kettering, inventive automotive genius. His credits among others include the invention of the self-starter and the development of the "Rocket engine."

Recently a new article appeared entitled "The Wonderful World of Charles F. Kettering" by T. A. Ward, condensed from *Professional Amateur*, a book being published by E. P. Dutton and Company. Mr. Ward tells us that Charles Kettering in his younger days came from a farm. He moved through a number of employment experiences before arriving in the world of automotive engineering.

He was in the primary grades at Big Run School, a country school in Ohio. Nearby stood Wolf's Mill. Charlie spent much time there watching the huge water wheel and learning something about this source of power. From the wise old miller he learned something else. "A lot of people are bound to worry," said the miller. "If you can do something about a problem, you ought to worry; but if you can't do anything, then worrying is like running the mill when there is no grist to grind. All that does is wear out the mill."

Few things are as crippling as worry. I do not recall the source and I cannot vouch for the accuracy of the figures, but it has been said that about 45 per cent of our objects of worry are in the past and cannot be changed, 38 per cent of our worries are over things in the present quite beyond our control and only 17 per cent are about things we can do something constructive about. Whatever the facts (and who can accurately measure this), worry remains as a strongly limiting factor for many.

Charles Kettering, it appears, learned something of value from the miller that day which has stayed with him for life. His philosophy is reflected in his methods of work. His uncommon success adds credence to the importance of a well-controlled "worry-department."

Controlled worry need not, however, be the prize of just a few. You, too, can keep this energy consumer in its proper place. The solution lies in intelligent thinking under God.

One of the secrets is to be found in the making of decisions. Vast numbers of people find this to be one of their most worrisome difficulties. Mrs. Franklin D. Roosevelt had a helpful answer when asked about her handling of manifold and difficult decisions. She replied that she tried to make the wisest decision on a matter that she could, then having made it, she stayed with it whatever the outcome.

The second secret is to determine which of the numbers of things that give us concern are in the past, and so beyond control, and eliminate them from further concern. What lies in the present, but beyond our control, should become a matter of prayer. Where our hand cannot reach, God's can.

Now the worrisome concerns about which we *can* do something remain. We then pray for courage to face the difficult, for wisdom to know the best, and for strength to accomplish the task. When there is "no grist to grind," we will be free. When there is "grist to grind," we will be strong.

Freedom, For What?

ONE DAY two incidents in the news gave me concern. The first was the story of a bomb scare in New York City. For some time the police had been trying frantically to turn up the "Mad Bomber."

Dynamite, however, can be found in more than a stick one can carry in his hand. A misuse of personal freedoms can be equally explosive. This brings me to the second story, which came out of Newark, New Jersey. Burlesque houses were crying the blues claiming that they had been robbed of their freedom of expression. They were no longer allowed to do as they pleased. In an attempt to regain their lost freedom, they were taking their case to the Supreme Court. The question to be debated would be, "What does the Fourteenth Amendment and freedom of expression really mean?"

In a questionnaire put to a large segment of the American public by the National Council of Churches this particular question was asked: "What are you thinking about?" One answer in reply was this: "What has happened to the American conscience?" We wonder sometimes, particularly in the realm of American morals.

Peculiar, is it not, that we do not call for freedom of expression when we drive down the highway? We may sometimes cross the yellow line through carelessness or deliberate foolishness. But we do not debate the common sense of the law against it. We come to a stop light, and on rare occasions even blindly go through it. But the law which says "No" we do not debate. A city health department sets up regulations governing the handling and distribution of foods. We assent to its ruling for the benefit of all. Building inspectors limit construction to certain well-defined requirements for safety. It is for the good of all and we accept it.

It is strange then that we find ourselves so freely debating the right and wrong of laws which relate to the world of morals.

We are brought to ask, does Christianity, does religion have anything to say about the moral dynamite in any community? Or are we to expect that there should be the freedom to express ourselves as we please in society irrespective of its relationship to other people?

A group of businessmen were sitting together in conversation one day talking about Christianity. One man said that he found that the inspiration of the church was very important in his life, but he added, "I want to be sure that my church and my pastor keep out of politics, society and the problems of the world because in the first place they don't know very much about it. Give me the simple gospel."

There was a minister in this group who said, "What do you mean when you talk about the simple gospel and wanting only that?" "Well," said the man, "I mean the simple gospel like old Amos, the prophet, used to preach in the Old Testament." The minister spoke up, "Do you remember the story of Amos? Amos was a country boy to begin with and came into town with a load of wool to sell. When he came into the market, he discovered that the buyers were crooks. They were cheating the sheep herders who were bringing in their wool. Amos proclaimed publicly before that community and nation the sin of cheating, of trying to buy somebody for a pair of shoes. Is that the man you meant?" said the minister. "I guess it must have been another one," was the reply.

God says, "Righteousness exalts a nation, but sin is a reproach to any people."

"Hear this, you who trample upon the needy
and bring the poor of the land to an end,
saying, 'When will the new moon be over,
 that we may sell grain?
And the sabbath,
 That we may offer wheat for sale,
That we may make the *measure* small and
 the money great,
 and deal deceitfully with false balances,
That we may buy the poor for silver
 and the needy for a pair of sandals
 and sell the refuse of the wheat'?"

It Takes Time "To Hatch"

IT IS A remarkable thing that in our modern age enough money and sufficient manpower can produce almost miraculous results in getting big things done in a big hurry. We Americans take an almost unholy pride in this. Many of our European friends would be tempted to declare that we have erected a god of energy and have fallen down to worship it. This, of course, may sound like a "sour grapes attitude." Yet it ought to lead us to an honest re-appraisal of our way of life.

An incident from the life of Charles F. Kettering, the automotive engineer, may help us here. Kettering had been working for some time to develop a drawer-operated cash register when one day he received some additional impetus from National Cash Register's president, John H. Patterson. Patterson was about to leave for Europe and "Ket" was asked whether the new register could be finished before the departure. Ket thought that it could. "We ought really to have it sooner," said Patterson. He directed that Kettering be given more help. "Give him twice as many men," he said, "so he can finish in half the time." At that, Kettering protested that he could not use so many helpers to advantage. "Why can't you?" asked Patterson. "If ten men can dig a rod of ditch in an hour, then surely twenty men can dig two rods." "This is more a job of hatching eggs than digging ditches, Mr. Patterson," Ket replied. "Do you think that if two hens were put on a nest, a setting of eggs could be hatched out in less than three weeks?"

It was a good question. It suggests to us in our rushed world that there are many things which simply cannot be raced to completion, fulfillment or success. Our problem is that we become unconscious victims of the spirit of getting big things done in a big hurry.

We know, for example, that a great scholar will not automatically be found at the end of an educational production line; that a great athlete is more than the product of co-ordination, muscle and skill under high-priced and high-pressured tutelage; that the greatest works of art are not produced "on order."

Nor do you and I become real persons of worth and quality to a friend or to the world as mere hurriers touching only the surface of things. Like a skipping stone across the mirrored face of a lake, we may leave only scattered circles of tiny ripples. The lake may remain relatively unchanged.

It takes time "to hatch," to develop an idea, to mature a mind, to deepen a friendship. We ought often to remove the halo from our gods of energy, speed and efficiency. We ought often to salute with new respect a measured quality to life, and only give a hurried tipping of our hats to slavish time.

The Wonder of You

A SIXTH GRADE teacher asked her class this question: What is here in the world today that was not here fifteen years ago? An unexpected surprise came in an answer from Johnny. His reply was simply, "Me." Of course he was right. Something wonderfully new came into the world when he was born, something God had planned and wanted.

It is easy for us to look beyond ourselves, to be awed by new inventions, new developments, quite unaware that one of the really important things that has happened is "me." Everything God has made has its own peculiar identity. There are billions of blades of grass and none of them alike. There are unnumbered snowflakes and none identical. But yet more exciting is the fact that there is no one else just like you. Even the prints of your fingers are separate and distinct. This ought to tell us something of our importance to God. It ought to lift us out of the doldrums when we feel that we do not count.

We are important. We may not, however, be important to the world for the same reasons. In the world of human society many measurements are used. Some people are beautiful or handsome, others homely. This may determine a starring role in a movie. Others are brilliant and of such intelligence as would make them geniuses. This may determine a position on a University faculty or in the world of politics. Some are particularly sensitive to the needs of others and have a high aptitude for guidance. This may place them high in the ranks of social service. Some are remarkably skilled with their hands. They may be among the creative artisans in useful production.

But these and all others are important for a reason greater than the attributes listed here. This basic importance traces to our being human personalities created by God and into which He has breathed a living, eternal soul.

The Psalmist, once astounded by this thought, expressed his appreciation of it in the words, "What is man that thou art mindful of him and the son of man that thou dost care for him? Yet thou hast made him little less than God . . ."

There is, however, an even deeper and more pointed evaluation made of man and it is this. God thought man worth saving from his own destructive self. He invaded humankind in the person of Jesus Christ, His Son, in order to make of a sinner a saint. He poured out His love to heal the spiritually sick, to mend the morally broken, to give sight to the inwardly blind. To such Christ comes to make a new people.

More remarkable yet, this Christ has chosen feeble humankind to be partners and workers together with Him in the refashioning of the world. No greater compliment was ever paid to men than this. "Ye are the salt of the earth." "Ye are the light of the world." Nor did He say this to a limited number blessed by dramatically skillful talents or superior intellects. He said it of what seem to be the most ordinary of men. And He has used these men in most unusual ways.

The Apostle Paul said, "For me to live is Christ." In this lay the secret of Paul's meaningfulness to the human race. In this will lie the secret of your importance to the Creator and to the world.

Faith on A Chaise Lounge

President Dwight D. Eisenhower spoke one day of tying a man's professed faith to his everyday activities. He suggested that the church should be telling the workman that the first demand his religion makes upon him is to be a good workman. If he is a carpenter, he should be a good carpenter. He should attend church by all means, but of what use is church if at the very center of life a man defrauds his neighbor and insults God by poor workmanship?

That is good thinking. If you and I believe what we profess, it ought to reflect itself in the common experiences of our everyday living. When it does, the world around us will take serious note of a professed Christian faith.

David S., a successful business man, an Episcopalian whose friendship I have valued, a man whom I have long admired, has told me in conversations we have had together, what it is like to be wrestling with Christian ethics in his highly competitive business world. His type of business is a thoroughly honorable one, but people with whom he deals are not always equally honorable. Some of them are determined to do business in a completely "cut-throat" style.

At least on one occasion Dave spoke his piece. He had worshipped together with the man on a Sunday morning. The following day Dave halted the attempted cut-throat conversation with this one question: "Do you want to do business today on the basis of what you professed and stood for yesterday morning as a Christian—or are you going to do business with me as though what we claim on Sundays has nothing to do with this deal? Just tell me straight so that I'll know what to expect."

Dave is not struggling with an isolated and ethereal problem in the business world. He has lots of company every day. Why is this so? Obviously there are many reasons. But certainly this is one of them: That there is an altogether too common a predisposition to compartmentalize one's religion so that it is isolated and insulated from the rest of one's life and the two are never brought together. One business man said, "What goes on in my church for an hour and fifteen minutes on Sunday morning has nothing to do with what goes on in business the rest of the week." He was not being critical. He was just stating a fact.

A greater tragedy than the existence of this situation is that we do not expect it to be any different. This, you see, is being contented to attend church regularly and then assume that this is all there is to Christianity. A general revival in religion across the nation is not enough, not when there is a corresponding increase in so many of the negatives that confront us every day on the American scene. The real need is to take Christ whom we worship on Sunday seriously enough to have our faith reflect itself through seven days of the week.

Christianity, if it is real on Sunday, should mean a going to work for God on Monday. Such a life is one where men understand that Christ did not come into the world just to make men "Chaise-lounge" comfortable on a quiet Sunday hour. He came to make new men in total life—home, job, business, love, politics, community, wherever we may be. He said clearly, "By this my Father is glorified, that you bear much fruit, and so prove to be my disciples."

Thinking About Yourself

IT WAS a gray day. The air was damp and chilly, not a day that you would ordinarily prescribe as ideal for a boat cruise on the lakes. But no one seemed to care. We were a group pleased with the opportunity for a few hours of relaxation after the strenuous weeks of the Lutheran World Assembly. One of the party seemed to concern himself even less with the weather than the others. He was seated on the back deck, reveling in the relaxing atmosphere, a ship captain's cap set jauntily on his head. He was Bishop Hanns Lilje, now beloved ex-president of the Lutheran World Federation.

During the days preceding, Bishop Lilje had attracted world-wide attention. Over a period of five years he had held the reins of the Federation, numbering fifty million Lutherans in 29 countries. Skilled as a parliamentarian, keen as a theologian, dynamic as a speaker, unparalleled as a diplomat, laurels were heaped one after another upon his head. Few men, world wide and in any field, match his abilities. Yet he is as humble and common as any man.

Gracious humility was a part of the Bishop wherever he was. During busy assembly days he would stop in the corridors of the church to thank a cleaning woman for her cheerful services. Again and again he would pause to tell his driver, the elevator operator, a secretary, or a waitress how much he appreciated their helpfulness.

Perhaps a most telling observation of his gracious humility was shown in this little incident on the cruise that day.

I had found in the cabin of the cruiser a current issue of *Time* magazine in which there was an article about the Assembly and its personalities. I handed it to Bishop Lilje and he scanned the paragraphs quickly. When he came to the direct reference to himself as a "stocky" German Bishop, he chuckled at the adjective. Reading on he found the phrases which described himself and other leaders as "ecclesiastical giants." With this, he rose to his feet, snapped to attention with a mock salute, then exclaimed with laughter how his homeland colleagues would snort with merriment were they to read this about him.

Bishop Lilje's reaction was like a refreshing breeze. Aware, no doubt, that he had been blessed by God with some abilities that had led to his position in the Christian Church, yet with a remarkably healthy spirit of gracious humility, he did not "think of himself more highly than he ought to think," as the great Apostle Paul once said. Our respected friend rather knew himself for just what he was, a sinner with a great Saviour. The Lord of the Church had been good enough to choose him and use him as one of his instruments in the Kingdom. The Bishop was a voice for God, not least a voice of gracious humility.

Truly "big people" are not those whose lives are measured alone by their position or rank in society. There are men and women of power and influence, perhaps even brilliant and dynamic personalities, who in many respects are still "little people" in spirit. Whatever a man's station in life, it is possible for him to have a healthy appraisal of himself. He will be lifted up because he knows that God loves him. He will be humbled in the realization that this love of God for himself is a reality in spite of his limitations. Few traits in Christian personality speak as effectively for God.

A Heart Full of Thanks

THERE IS A little chuckle in this story. I found it in a news letter entitled "Perspective," printed by Dick Halverson, a friend of mine. The story goes like this: A Communist is reporting to his superior officer. He has just returned from a government mission to the United States. It is a tragic picture that he paints. "America is desperate for food. Her people have taken to the last resources of a starving nation. They are killing their dogs and eating them. And this fact is so well known that no attempt at concealment is made. At a baseball game I attended," he went on, "vendors in white jackets passed among the spectators shamelessly offering sandwiches of dog meat for sale and crying out, 'Hot Dogs!' Moreover, they were snatched up at such speed as to indicate general starvation."

Quite apparently this is only a story. No visitor to the United States could possibly convince himself of the truth of such a pictured desperation. The fanciful story is good for a laugh. The truth is good for some serious consideration and oft forgotten gratitude.

No nation in all the world has been more abundantly favored than our own America. In the United States we have a billion acres of farm land. Five hundred million acres of forests cover our hills. Beneath the soil are to be found a hundred million acres of coal, iron, copper and other minerals. Thirty-four million acres of rivers and lakes dot or traverse our landscape. We have a hundred million acres of developed city land, three hundred and sixteen thousand oil wells, six million five hundred thousand farms, two million miles of railroad, two hundred and fifty thousand miles of electric transmission lines and ever increasing millions of radios and television sets.

With only 7% of the world's population we have 80% of the cars, 50% of the telephones and 20% of the world's beef production. We have one radio for every three people. Russia has one for every ninety. It is not a strange fact to us that the average American enjoys more and better food as well as better housing; wears more and finer clothing; and possesses more comforts and conveniences than the average citizen of any other country.

It is at the close of another day that a re-appraisal of such facts as these leads us to a renewed sense of gratitude. Surely God has richly and daily provided us with more than any nation and people could ask for—"for all of which I am in duty bound to thank and praise, to serve and obey Him." This is most certainly true in theory. It ought to be true in practice. You and I can help to make it so.

Puppet Thinking

W HO DOES your thinking for you? That is a peculiar question, I know. But it is a good one.

A somewhat unusual car-train accident took place some years ago. A long line of cars held impatient drivers who were waiting for the train to pass and the crossing to clear. The signal lights flashed red with prolonged regularity. Suddenly the last railroad car flashed by, but the signal lights continued their staccato beat in the darkness. The driver of the lead car held his place though his good judgment played to the accompaniment of a noisy symphony of horns blasting behind him. He hesitated a moment. He remembered that more than one set of tracks crossed the road. But, pressured by the impatient scolding from other drivers, he yielded his best judgment, shifted into gear and moved directly into the path of a second train which came out from behind the first. There was a metal-rending crash, then silence; and another fatality was listed on the state's record books. Under pressure the driver had allowed others to do his thinking for him.

Many other areas of life are affected in the same way. Some years ago when I spoke to a Parent-Teacher's Congress, a great number of questions were asked and discussed following the address. One of the questions asked was this one posed by a mother. "What do we do when our children come home with some special request which we think wise to deny, but then hear by way of rebuttal, 'Well, Jane's mother thinks it is all right.'?" She added, "This is the kind of thing we are faced with all the time." I agreed that this was a real problem. My wife and I having wrestled with that one, too. The answer, of course, lies in parents having to use their best judgment in making the best decision of which they are capable, not on the basis of another's thinking but on the basis of their own.

Nor is the problem existent only in parental relationships. You find it in your office, within your community, in your choice of recreation and amusement. Take a stand for what you believe in and it is more than likely that you may catch the reply, "Don't be a stuffed shirt. Everybody's doing it." Every one of us knows down deep that this cannot be the intelligent measurement of right or wrong. Our decisions cannot simply be decisions of the majority, or decisions of pressure.

The Apostle Paul was well aware of this problem as the Christian confronted it. On one occasion he said, "Do not be conformed to this world, but be transformed by the renewal of your mind . . ." Somewhere man must find a ruling factor for his life. A million voices clamor for our attention and allegiance. Which voice shall it be? Who will be your guide? Shall it be another as inadequate and weak as you may be? Or shall it be One who knows all, who speaks and willingly guides the listening ear?

Friend, let God rule your life. Do not be a puppet on someone else's string. Live close to Him. You can know His will. Let Him be the guiding factor in your life.

Doing As You Please?

A YOUNG MAN sat in my office one evening, his otherwise handsome face marred by a frown. He had been telling me the story of his unhappy, frustrated and mixed-up life. Everything had come out wrong. There had been a job, a firing, another job and another firing. There had been a marriage, a divorce, another marriage and that was a failure, too. There had been drinking, some sobriety, more drinking, an accident, hospital bills and more trouble. He concluded, "I just cannot understand why life always turns out all wrong for me. This isn't true for everybody, so why for me?"

"Suppose I try to explain with this illustration," I suggested. "You have bought a new car. You drive it out of the garage and down the street. You have a fine sense of pride as you listen to the smooth purring of the motor under the hood. The brakes take hold efficiently when they are applied. The finish has a high polish and shows off a beautiful two-tone color. Your pickup going away from a traffic light throws you against the back of the seat.

"You bring your car to a stop in front of your house. For a few minutes you sit appreciatively absorbing the sensation of satisfaction. Then with a bit of curiosity you pull from the glove compartment an operating manual prepared by the manufacturer. It contains suggestions and sound rules for good car care—a certain air pressure in your tires, a good grade of gasoline, regular oil changes, anti-freeze for your radiator in cold weather, these and many others, each of them important.

"But you say to yourself, 'This is my car. No one is going to tell me how to run it. I will carry whatever air pressure I like in my tires. I will use cheap gasoline and save some money. I will just add oil, not change it. I will grease the car when I feel like it. It is my car and I will do as I please with it.' "

I then said to the young man, "This is your privilege. It is your car to do with as you please. But suppose that you do as you please, ignoring the directives of the manufacturer. What will be the result? You will have kept your independence and pride, but you will have wrecked your car. It will be a mechanical cripple. Nor will you be surprised."

The young man sat back with a thoughtful expression on his face as I continued. "Does it now seem at all peculiar to you that your life has turned out as it has? You, too, have a Creator, a Designer. He is the Almighty God. He knows far more about us as His creation than we know about ourselves. He knows how we must live if life is to come out right. He has given us a manual of operations, too—the Ten Commandments. He did this not to satisfy his ego but because He loves us and wants the best for us, both for time and for eternity. Our God says, 'Whatever a man sows, that he will also reap.' That is the way life works both positively and negatively, both with the pluses and the minuses.

"But how will you be able to choose rightly, to live obediently? This requires a power that is beyond your own. It is the power of God. It is Jesus Christ, man's Saviour who can take hold of your heart and make you a new person with a new will. It is He who can lead you to obedient living. This begins when you have been led to humbly say, 'I have played the fool. I have sinned aganst my God.' It begins there, but it ends with your coming to love to do the will of God and finding God's blessing in it. It is then that life comes out right—doing not as you please but as pleases Christ."

The Risk In Love

"Maybe she sees something that we don't see." These were the thought-provoking words of appraisal made by a doctor in the corridor of the Cook County Hospital in Chicago. Each evening for more than twenty months something quietly dramatic had occurred in that hospital room. On the bed lay John Brookhouse, thirty-six years old, a cab driver, victim of a back alley slugging. His eyes were wide open, but by any possible medical measurements he was wholly unconscious.

"Hello, John, how are you tonight?" Ann Brookhouse, his wife, would ask as she entered the room each evening. Then, sitting at John's bedside, she would rehearse the happenings of the day. She would tell about their son, John, Jr., fifteen, and their daughters, June, thirteen years old, and Alvina, just turned twelve. It was wholly a one-way conversation but on Ann's part as animated as though they were both deeply involved in it.

Quite naturally the doctors and nurses were puzzled by the unusual drama taking place in that room. To their best knowledge John was engulfed in a deep coma beyond the possibility of either hearing or understanding. Ann's recital of the day's events seemed utterly futile. And yet, the doctor in the corridor made this observation: "Maybe she sees something that we don't see."

Love does have unexplainable qualities and characteristics. The expression of love does not always follow the pattern of logic and reason. It cannot be measured by mathematical formula. Without any conscious reception of it love is often expressed in a constant flow of self-giving by one to another. Often love involves a great risk and demands the payment of a high price in sacrifice and devotion. To the casual observer this may appear to border on the ridiculous. The actions of Ann Brookhouse may have seemed so. But the doctor, skilled in more than the medically technical, was wise enough to see beyond. The key lay in the far-seeing eye of love.

And how else can man seek even in the simplest of ways to explain the actions of God toward man? The practical and the logical do not explain the love of the Almighty and Holy One for finite, sinful man. Man himself finds it difficult and often impossible to love his unlovely counterparts in his fellow men. Yet God loves. He sees what we do not see. And He deemed it worthwhile that His own Son Jesus Christ should at the greatest of prices, a cross, seek to win the hearts of the indifferent, the unlovely, the rebellious. It is beyond us to explain.

To explain such love is impossible. Nor, as we look at it, is it necessary. But to accept such love is possible. God by His Spirit has made it so. The road may be a long one for God. But He sees something we do not see for He is love itself. Nor did He count the risk of His Son's life too great a price to pay in order to win our love in return. No man will love God simply because He ought to. He will love God when His heart is won by the unfathomable self-giving love of Christ.

The Bark On The Inside

As seething undercurrents in an ocean finally dash themselves against ship or shore, so the angry undercurrents of a human soul strike at fellow beings with disastrous results.

A newlywed of Cleveland, Ohio, found herself the object of such anger and recently stumbled into a Los Angles hospital accusing her husband, William, of cutting her hair and beating her while on their honeymoon.

Readers Digest once carried a little squib that went something like this. A woman had been bitten by a mad dog. Critically ill, she was advised by her doctor that she might not live and perhaps she ought to write her last wishes. She spent a long time with pencil and paper. Finally her doctor remarked about the length of the will she was writing. "Will!" she snorted, "This isn't a will. I am writing a list of the people I would like to bite."

There is some humor in that story and we chuckle a bit until we realize that this woman was saying very honestly what a great number of people feel much of the time. We might be quite surprised at the traffic jam on our streets if everyone carrying a grudge and living with sharp animosity were to get into his car and drive to do to another what he feels like doing. The drivers of those cars would include a vast section of human society. There would be husbands and wives, ex-husbands and ex-wives, parents and children, brothers and sisters, employers and employees, associates and neighbors.

I sat one day in juvenile court. The young man seated before the judge was in grave trouble. Father and mother, separated and estranged, sat at one side. Even in the midst of the court hearing this couple, who had once pledged their troth in a marriage vow, were audibly heard criticizing each other and firing sharp arrows of bitterness and resentment. There was nothing of a forgiving spirit. Over the years a victim of it all had been this son.

Many hatreds and animosities, however, are not obvious on the outside. Yet they are present like smouldering fires ready to break into full flame. They create tensions, frustrations and heartaches which destroy the human spirit. Like an iceberg, whether above or below surface, they endanger the traffic lanes of everyday life.

A child was walking along a street when a large dog came out barking at her. She stood frozen in her tracks, terrified. Soon a stranger came to her rescue. "Come, little girl. The dog has stopped barking," said the man. "Yes," she said, "but I can see the bark is still on the inside." She still saw in the eyes of the dog an unfriendly spirit.

The attempt to simply submerge or control antagonisms is not the answer, as witness a certain woman who said that she could rid herself of her severe headaches only when she learned how to forgive. Only forgiveness will cleanse and renew the human spirit troubled by anger and bitterness. Such forgiveness does not come naturally, however. It comes in the experience of a man with his Lord in being himself forgiven. Something is learned here. A new spirit is born. The bark is gone.

A Voice For God

"I will never forget his face." "I wish that there were something I could do for him." "It is as though he had been through so much that nothing could really hurt him any more." These are statements which came from the lips of a waitress, a doctor and a business man. They were speaking of Bishop Ordass of Hungary.

It was at the Lutheran World Federation Assembly in Minneapolis that Bishop Ordass made such an indelible impression upon thousands of Americans and hundreds of overseas delegates. His message was direct and penetrating even in his slowly moving English. His already publicized experiences behind the iron curtain acted as a backdrop on a stage and set off each word in bold relief. Even the overflow audiences beyond the sight of his person sat in rapt attention. Here was a man who had defied the edicts of the Communists, had refused to bend his will to the will of the state. For many months he had been the object of attempted brain-washing in the aloneness of a solitary confinement cell. Years of "house arrest" followed. All of this was persecution in modern dress.

Few if any men that I have known have ever made such an impact upon so many. There is in this Hungarian Bishop a mingling of many traits. Two of these appear to be in sharp contrast. One side of his personality evidences the warmest of human spirits, another a hard-core courage.

I shall never forget his warmth and tenderness. It showed itself so clearly when for two and one half hours one day he occupied my office following a Hungarian communion service. During that period fellow Hungarians, many of them refugees, took their turns for a few brief moments with him. Never have I seen so many tears shed as when they spoke with him of loved ones, victims of the October 1956 revolt. They were tears shed by grown men and women on the shoulder of a warm-hearted spiritual father.

Or, I recall, and I suspect my daughters will never forget, the times when he put his arms around them, stooped with a kiss and took up permanent residence in their affectionate hearts. Nor shall I ever forget when he spoke of the church, my congregation, and my family, then took me gently by the arm and said, "How very much blessed you are."

But this is not all for, contradictory as it may seem to some, this man of deep love and tenderness was also a man of remarkable courage. There was little of his personal experience to which he himself referred publicly. The press had told his story. His audience, well aware of it, felt his simple message of Christian faith fall like a thunder clap upon their ears. This was not demonstrative bravado, an attempt to convince himself or others of that which rested fearfully within his own soul. Rather it was the witness of a courage tested in the crucible of twentieth century persecution.

The shadows of an ominous future seemed to settle over his shoulders again when he sat at dinner with our family on the last day of his visit. Yet the glow of his radiant faith shone through as he talked about his past life in solitary confinement. "Yet," he said, "I was never alone." Then he told of what it had meant to be able to recite from memory whole chapters of the Bible, sometimes in Swedish, or in English, or in his native tongue. This, he said, was the secret defense against the attempts to drive him mad.

It was now to an unknown and hazardous future that the Bishop was to return. But of this future he spoke in these carefully chosen words. "I am not afraid. If I go to the worst, I will go with joy."

His was a voice for God.

What Do You Make of It?

E. Studdard Kennedy, the famous British chaplain of World War I, while chatting one day with an acquaintance, found himself confronted by this most unusual question—"Kennedy, what do you think the Almighty is going to ask you on Judgment Day?" Kennedy, as I am told the story, paused, showed some perplexity, and then replied, "I am not at all sure what the Almighty is going to ask me on Judgment Day, but I would not be too surprised if He were simply to look at me, and ask, 'Well, Kennedy, what did you make out of it?' "

Perhaps Kennedy envisioned a longer statement from the Lord which might have been like this: "Kennedy, you have been one of my created beings. You were given life with breath to breathe, eyes to see, ears to hear, talents and abilities to use and a mind to think. In addition to this and all that you have found in the world surrounding you, you were also given an eternal soul. Your Creator God was made known to you. His will and purpose was revealed to you. His love in the gift of Jesus Christ, His Son and your Savior, you knew. Kennedy, what did you make out of it?"

I do not know what the Almighty God is going to ask of me on Judgment Day. You do not know either. But I would not be too shocked or surprised if He were to ask something quite similar to the question posed to E. Studdard Kennedy. And I think it might be wise to ask myself today what my response might be. Far better to check with the conductor when the train leaves the depot than at the end of the line,—

particularly if you are on the wrong train, going in the wrong direction.

Not all of us, however, are wise enough to do this kind of thinking voluntarily and by choice. How often such important moments of self-analysis come only with the stress of enforced illness, idleness or pressuring heartache. Many pastors can not tell about people who in early, middle or late life have indicated a deep gratitude for their "detour" experiences. Pain, financial loss, fears, and discomfort may have been theirs. But the gain was worth the price. They had stopped long enough in life's mad scramble to ask themselves a most important question, "What am I making out of it?"

There are no rewards of value at the end of life when such a life is lived falsely. It was Jesus who said of one whose sole concern was for building bigger and better barns, —"Fool! This night your soul is required of you, and the things you have prepared, whose will they be?"

"What did you make out of it?" It is something of great value when a man can reply, "I have found Him who said, 'I am come that you might have life and have it more abundantly.'"

Don't Hate Yourself

"**I** hate myself for being so mean to you." This phrase, you may recall, was the opening line in a popular song some thousand "Hit Parades" ago. Whether the song writer realized it or not, he was touching on a more common experience than one to be found alone in the world of romance. When you are mean to another, you usually find yourself rather unhappy about you.

There is a switch to this thought which is also often true with equally great damage. A title for this song might be "Because I hate myself, I'm being so mean to you." Are you surprised? This is a very common experience. Thousands of people dislike themselves very much. Because they do, they dislike other people. They may not, however, be aware of this at all.

A young lady came to my office for counsel. She was a professing Christian, held a splendid position and desired to be a fine Christian person. "But," she said, "I feel spiritually dead inside. I do not love God as I ought. I do not really love others." It developed that she was all wrapped up in herself. She lived behind a respectable appearing front but was regularly nervous, irritable and depressed.

When we had spent some time talking, we together made some helpful discoveries. In a concerned self-appraisal, the young lady found that she had been carrying a rather unhealthy sense of pride over the impeccable life she was displaying for others to see. But it was a false pride and based on a false premise. Actually she disliked herself very much and was anything but proud of what she had once done and been. She had for some time confessed her past sins and sought to be forgiven. But she was not sure that God had forgiven her. At any rate she had not forgiven herself, whatever the promises and assurances she had from God. She still hated herself as much as in the days when her gross misconduct had been a constant part of her disturbed but impenitent life. Only when it was possible for her to trust in God's forgiving love for sinners was it possible for her to forgive herself as well.

None of us can hate ourselves and find it easy to like or to live cordially with others. When this hate of self exists, we cannot be natural. We must build a wall of defense and keep a little distance. We do not want others to see us as we really are. This is our thinking, however unconsciously it develops. A fine facade may be built, but the real you is lost in a maze of hidden inner rooms.

There is a key which will unlock the door to hidden rooms. There is a power which will blast away a false front and build new and handsomely. The key is the forgiving love of Jesus Christ for every sinner. The power to build new again is the power of the Holy Spirit, which power can make you a new person in Christ. Made clean in the eyes of God, we can be made clean in the eyes of men and in our own eyes. Then we can stop with pretenses. We can "be ourselves in Christ." No longer are we then lost in ourselves for we can quit concentrating our thoughts there. Life now is centered on Christ and on others. Life becomes an adventure for we are the real persons God intended us to be.

Keep Your Heart Up

K EEP YOUR CHIN up! Would it not be wonderful if it could be done as easily as one can say it? Is anything more maddening for a human soul than to be told "keep your chin up" when, however hard you may try, at that moment you simply cannot do so.

I sat one day at a hotel-room desk in Cleveland preparing an address to be given that evening. Late in the afternoon I wanted to stretch my legs. But it was not a day for walking. A cold rain swept across the city square. Then I remembered the long lobbies and the maze of ramps and corridors which led from the Hotel Cleveland through the terminal building adjacent to it, down to the subways and trains, out and under streets to banks, department stores and other centrally located facilities. I started on my way.

As I strode up a ramp toward the street entrance my attention was fixed on a man entering whose face was bent so low that all I could see was the top of his hat. I expected momentarily that he would look up. He did not. He continued toward me, past me, on down the ramp to the subway. I had not seen as much as his chin. But as he passed by I saw that a physical deformity had forced this man's head into such a position. All that he could see was the front of his coat, his shoes, the floor of the corridor below him and the shoes and feet of others who passed close by. He was, I suspect, an un-

witting authority on shoes—shined and unshined—pins, lost
pennies, scrap paper, curbs, thresholds and the like. For all
that he could see, people were feet, buildings were floors and
rain was a puddle. A man's heart goes out to someone like
that.

I wish that I had been given the opportunity to meet and
know that man. I may be all wrong but it is quite possible
that my unknown friend, though physically deformed, was
not one bit "out-of-shape" in spirit. I can imagine him saying,
"Don't feel sorry for me. It is true that I have my chin forced
down against my collar-bone. I really have to work at it in
order to be able to get a good look around me. But there are
folks worse off than I am. There is a man who has the chin
of his spirit hanging very low. He cannot see anything around
about him either. He is an authority only on reflected sunshine, on penny-size hopes, pin-size dreams, curbs on his ambitions, scraps of success and the dirt of frustration. It is he
who is far worse off than I for I can *hold my heart up*."

It is a hard thing to lose your spirit, to have your courage
run away. It is a fearful thing to have the normal task become
a giant wall, to have self-confidence melt away in the gloom.
It is a depressing thing not to care, to let life go.

"Keep your chin up." Regardless of language, phrase or
idiom, this has been a word of encouragement from friend to
friend over the centuries. But, however well meant, there
must be more than casual words to lift chins off the floor, to
put a new lilt in one's voice, a new bounce in one's stride. In
days long past when Psalmists knew the hovering gloom of
heavy hearts, one said, "But as for me my feet had almost
stumbled, my steps had well-nigh slipped . . . But when I
thought how to understand this, it seemed to be a wearisome

task, until I went into the sanctuary of God; then understood I . . . " Another Psalmist added, "I lift up my eyes to the to the hills. From whence does my help come? My help comes from the Lord who made heaven and earth."

It is the Lord who can keep a man's heart up. It is He who helps a mind to think, a hand to work and a heart to pray. Then out of gloom comes sunshine and a new tomorrow.

Why Not Fall In Love?

IF YOU FEEL like a misunderstood outsider in this crazy-quilt world, maybe you need to fall in love. It is that over-flowing, self-giving attitude which has been prescribed as the radical healing needed for the inner frustrations of modern life. This prescription was written into a report following a two-year church study by a National Council of Churches committee examining the insecurities and discontents of our age.

The report did not use these exact words but George Cornell, the Associated Press religious news writer, indicated that the blissful exuberance and sweet surrender of falling in love with another human being might well indicate the cure needed,—a falling in love with God. "It is being drawn to another in faith and faithful love. The response," the report says, "is not an achievement for which you can claim credit, not a calculated decision and not a moral attainment any more than falling in love is any of these things. Self-giving is involved in it as in love or loyalty," the report adds, "but the decision is caused by an irresistible love. You can do no other."

Such a love for God is a real need in our world. Ours is a world in which can be found a rash of pagan gospels of race, class and national aggrandizement propagated through the mass media of our day. These, the report adds, are decrying gentleness and meekness, fomenting distrust and conflict, and appealing all too effectively to men's self-interest and their deep craving for companionship, emotional security, self-respect and some higher power to serve.

It is against such a background that there has developed on the American scene a conscious resurgence of evident spiritual need and concern. Many people, long indifferent or even hostile to the voices for Christianity, are now listening and hoping to find some answers to needs not found elsewhere. It is perhaps startling to many to discover that Jesus Christ does not hand out pat answers nor commonly desired rewards to those who look to Him. He never did promise "success" as we think of it. Rather, by contrast, He promised a share in His own life of toil and victorious suffering. He promised the strength of a humble mind and the joy of an unshakable trust in God.

A great soldier of distant years and distant places stood one day for long moments in the corridor of a great cathedral. In the days of his boyhood his heart had been touched by the person of Christ. Now for long years he had kept Christ on the fringe areas of his life. Once again he confronted the Christ in a striking painting in oil which hung on the wall above him. It showed Christ dying on a cross to save and win the hearts of men. Slowly the soldier sank to his knees where with bowed head he whispered over and over again, "From now on it will be for Him, only Him."

"We love because he first loved us." This is the spark which leads a man to fall in love with God. Sinner that he is, he finds in Christ's love for him the power to love the Christ. Then amidst the tensions and fears of a world at cold war with God, the Christian glows with spiritual warmth in love of God.

Adventure In Living

HOW DOES THE WORD "adventure" fit into the setting of our modern day? Has not our well established society, our rather comfortable mechanized world removed from our doors the opportunity for adventure? Is not life pretty well stabilized? Are not the frontiers of life rather remote?

Such questions are understandable when we think about "adventure." That word has been relegated for the most part to the covers of pulp magazines and to the descriptive paragraphs in our television or movie columns describing a western. For most of us the word "adventure" applied to daily life has become a rather puzzling misnomer. It does seem to be part of the "frontier's day" past. Yet, I wonder if this is really true provided we understand the meaning of the word "adventure."

Webster defines it as "the encountering of risks; hazardous enterprise, a bold undertaking in which hazards are to be met and the issue hangs upon unforeseen events; a daring feat, a remarkable experience,—to venture or hazard oneself; as adventuring upon paths unknown . . ." This is the meaning of adventure.

It is apparent that there have been changes in the areas in which we adventure today in contrast to yesterday. Yet there is a great deal more of adventure in our day than we may think. Some of it is more dramatic than Lewis and Clark crossing the Rockies. It is true that little of it has to do with horses and guns, or forests and storms. Most of it has nothing to do with hostile enemies lurking in the brush. And yet there is high adventure with the encountering of risks and challenging them, hazardous enterprises tackled and successfully met.

Our young people still have it. The high school junior lifts his foot onto a locker room bench and ties the laces on his football shoes with tense and nervous fingers. Adventure lies beyond that door where the band is playing and the cheers are rocking the stands.

A salesman enters a potential customer's place of business. A competing line of goods is already established in the store. Will he be able to sell the dealer his line, perhaps so successfully as to even replace the competitor entirely? This is adventure.

The business man risks the opening of a new store. The young executive gambles on a change of companies and takes a risk for a new opportunity. An advertising man dreams a new product promotion. A teacher tries a new class method. A fisherman whittles a new plug.

But there is also adventure elsewhere. You too can find it. Where, you ask? Ours is in many respects a troubled world. There is a great deal of heartache and gloom. But there is a field for adventure in helping to lift some of the blanket of gloom and pessimism. Nor do you need to be a TV comic, or on the other hand, a United Nations delegate to achieve this spirit of adventure. You need only be where you are, suddenly caught up in the life adventure of outgoing and overpowering "kindliness."

That sounds desperately oversimplified, I know. But have you ever really adventured here? If you have not, you will be amazed. More loneliness, jealousy, aimlessness, hopelessness and heart-hunger are dispelled as a result of kindliness than you can imagine. A giving of yourself brings amazing results. Ralph Waldo Emerson said, "Rings and jewels are not gifts but apologies for gifts. The only gift is a portion of thyself." A French proverb states, "He gives nothing who does not give himself."

Try adventuring in kindliness. There is no shortage of frontiers here. And done in the name of Christ, each act of kindness becomes a holy act. Jesus said, . . . "as you did it to one of the least of these my brethren, you did it to me."

"A World Gone Sane"

"A WORLD GONE SANE." What would such a world of human beings be like? This is the startling question by H. G. Wells in *Star Begotten*, his book published in 1937. World War II was just around the corner. Turn that corner and the question would still have been a good one. Turn more corners, come to our day, and the question is still more thought-provoking.

Look back at the succession of recent years and remind yourself of a number of world-shaking events that have transpired. In a five-year period Germany disappeared as a great nation, Japan ceased to exist as a world power, the atomic age was ushered in, Russia emerged from centuries of political eclipse to become a first-class world power. Any one of these would make a stimulating epoch in a period of one hundred years.

Add to that period the days in which we now live. Russia exchanges blunt and dire threats with us over the establishment of air bases in Holland, over so-called "meddling" in the Middle and Near East; South Korea requests atomic war equipment to match that of her counterpart to the North. "A world of human beings gone sane." What would that be like? How wonderful if we could find out!

Our "insanities," however, are not alone to be found in

distant places so that at home we may easily brush aside
personal responsibility and piously adjust our halos. The
poet Carl Sandburg on a recent birthday morning ate his
scrambled eggs and then deplored, for press consumption,
the American manner of pursuing happiness. He said that the
result of our pursuit was a fat, dripping prosperity but that
when the goal of a country is only happiness and comfort,
there is danger. Albert Einstein said as much,—"To make a
goal of comfort or happiness has never appealed to me." He
wanted the element of struggle in life. To this thought Carl
Sandburg added, "Before you go to sleep at night you say,
'I haven't got it yet. I haven't got it yet.' Take the man who
invented the thermostat blanket. I hope he did not say to
himself, 'Now I'll go to Florida and sit around.' "

We cannot afford such thinking either. "We haven't got it
yet." What the creator God intended our world to be and
what we have made of it hold little similarity. The problem
lies in our souls and spirits.

Will you press these thoughts between the leaves of your
mind for a few days? See what comes of it. The thoughts are
these: If you had the soul of a Shakespeare within you, how
you could write! If you had the spirit of a Beethoven in you,
how you could compose! If you had the soul of MacArthur,
how you could lead! But add this, most important of all,—
if you had the spirit of Christ in you, how you could live!
Multiply this by the sum total of us,—how we as a nation
and world could live,—sanely.

> "A tender child of summers three
> Seeking her little bed at night
> Paused on the dark stair timidly,
> 'O, Mother, take my hand,' said she,
> 'And then the dark will all be light.'

"We older children probe our way
From dark behind to dark before
And only when our hand we lay,
Dear Lord, in Thine, the night is day
And there is darkness nevermore."

"Striving After Wind'

YOU MAY CALL it a foot-feed, a gas-pedal, or accelerator, but by whatever name one young man put too heavy a foot on it for too long. Twice warned against speeding, the young man, less than two hours after the second warning, carried himself and four others to death in a two-car accident.

This, however, is not the only modern setting where one sees a dangerous heavy-footed race through life. Some years ago a friend, the owner-executive of a very large business, headed for the Mayo Clinic in Rochester, Minnesota, for a thorough check-up. He had not been walking with his formerly buoyant step. Some of the laughter had gone out of his voice. At the clinic he received a very thorough examination. The verdict given him was that there was nothing organically wrong. He had simply been pushing too hard. His orders were to return home and take his heavy foot off the foot-feed.

A recent survey of 142 executives in large corporations showed that an unusually large number of them had heart trouble, advanced cases of ulcers and other symptoms of illness resulting from pressure and tension. It was further concluded in a special study of one $100,000-a-year man that he could almost assume that he would be dead in another ten years at his present work-and-worry rate.

This group, however, does not hold the exclusive rights

to this cult of foolishness. There are a great many in less glittering brackets who are also "caught up" in the same modern American whirlpool of push, rush and success.

Some of this may grow out of a philosophy of indispensability that may be rooted more deeply in us than we imagine. It is as though the world would suffer tomorrow if we were merely to slow down to normal today. The compulsion to rush and press also may be urged on us even more strongly by the spirit of our age. A European visitor to America once asked why we did not erect a statue to the god of energy in a public square and fall down to worship it. He was struck by what seemed to him a total imbalance in our values. He saw scores of otherwise intelligent people rather unintelligently priding themselves in long hours and overly strenuous activities in order to "succeed."

Go back to the writer of the Old Testament book Ecclesiastes. He says, "I hated all my toil in which I had toiled under the sun, seeing that I must leave it to the man who will come after me; and who knows whether he will be a wise man or a fool . . . Better is a handful of quietness than two hands full of toil and striving after wind."

Quite strangely, this dangerous driving mood of our day has a counterpart equally as destructive of society and of the individual human spirit. Its focal point is seen in the lazy and irresponsible who are caught up in a dream world of unearned security. Often able-bodied and of average to better-than-average mentalities, they are nevertheless the parasites or barnacles, the "free-loaders" in the economic scheme. These ride through life with a foot on the brake—encouraging others to buy the gas, to press the foot-feed . . . "It is God's gift to man that everyone should eat and drink and take pleasure in all his toil."

Holy Scripture states that:

"For everything there is a season, and a time for every matter under heaven:

a time to be born, and a time to die;

a time to plant, and a time to pluck up what is planted;

a time to break down, and a time to build up;

a time to weep, and a time to laugh;

a time to mourn, and a time to dance;

a time to cast away stones, and a time to gather stones together;

a time to seek, and a time to lose;

a time to keep, and a time to cast away;

a time to rend, and a time to sew. . . ."

Man Of God

IT WAS AFTER dark that I was walking through Denny Park in Seattle, Washington. The city was my birthplace and the park an area not too far from the neighborhood where I had pulled my wagon. The congregation into which I had been born was now located in a newer structure across the street.

Near the south entrance to the park I found a pedestal upon which stood the bust of a man honored by the community. In the gloom he appeared to be an almost Lincolnesque figure with sharp features and flowing hair. I lit a match to read the dedicatory inscription below and found, if I recall them correctly, these words: MARK A. MATTHEWS, Man of God and Friend of the People.

The story may be strange to you. Mark A. Matthews was a minister, described to me as a tall, gaunt man, striking in appearance and of such courage and devotion to his God and to his community that he made one of the greatest contributions to the city of Seattle ever made by any man in any walk of life.

"Man of God." How rarely that title is used in our day even including those whose chosen profession finds them constantly within the framework of the Church. The fault is our own as pastors. Too many scattered efforts in seeking to meet too many varied demands have often made us less than strong men of God. Procrastinating in that which is most critical and urgent, we have often given time and energy to the less important activities in the plans and purposes of God.

But this is not alone of critical concern for pastors with pulpits. Each layman ought as well to be first and foremost a "man of God." And there are thousands of dedicated Christian men and women in America. Whether "doctor, lawyer, merchant, chief," they are first men and women of God. Whether "tinker, tailor, soldier, sailor," they are first and by choice "men and women of God." They have not succumbed to what may well be Satan's cleverest ruse.

Once upon a time, so the legend goes, Satan asked his helpers to propose ways and means of breaking up a spiritual revival on earth. One suggested, "I would tell the people that there is no God, no devil, no heaven, no hell, and that they should eat, drink and be merry for tomorrow we die." "You need not go," said Satan. "No one would believe you."

A more shrewd assistant said, "Let me go and tell them that the Bible is a good book, but that it is only partially true. I would tell them that there is a God and a heaven but no devil and no hell and that, no matter how they lived, they would be eternally happy." But Satan said, "Only a minority would believe that."

Finally the shrewdest said, "I would tell them the Bible is all true and that they must make their choice between God and Satan but that there is no hurry," "Good," said Satan. "You have the system."

This strange procrastination of ours has new facets to it but it is basically as old as the human race and the fall of man. "The Man of Distinction," "The Organization of Man,"

"The Man of the Year," "The Successful Man," "The Influential Man," "The Community Man" and all the rest may be phrased terminology out of the Twentieth Century but their counterparts under other titles have occupied their pedestals in unnumbered societies through the ages. Only rarely has the title "Man of God" held import. Only rarely has the spiritual held a priority position in the minds of men except in hour of crisis and of fear. But it was "Man of God" first, then "Friend of the People," which described the Man of all men and the Friend of all friends,—Jesus Christ. It was He who said "Seek ye *first* the Kingdom . . ."

The Tyranny Of Success

W E BEGIN with some seventy-five cent words. Two of them are coined words which can be traced to Howard Whitman. He was writing about success and the dangers involved in a wrong understanding of its meaning. He said that some people have arteriosclerosis because of "materiosclerosis"; they are driven to serious heart ailments because of a love of things with a constant pressure to attain them. Others confused in their understanding of success have arteriosclerosis because of "superiorsclerosis"; their heart conditions develop as a result of over-reaching for superiority.

Someone has said that there is nothing new under the sun and I suspect that this problem of mispriced life values is as old as most. However old or new a problem, a re-evaluation here is important. Professor Mandel Sherman of the University of Chicago thought so and recently made a two-year study of success. In his conclusions he said this, "The common idea is that to be successful a man must be superior to others in riches, in power, in social position and that he is frustrated if he is not." Perhaps we need a new definition. It might read like this, suggested Dr. Sherman: "Success means that we are inwardly stimulated to do the best we can by the love of doing what we are capable of doing." He goes on to say that the successful person is not upset by the competition of others. Your success has really nothing to do with someone else's success. You use your own talents and do your best. Also, being at the top is not necessarily success. It may mean that you have become just a core, a dried-up driver, a mechanical sort of personality.

Dr. Sherman's thoughts take me back to one of the most successful people I have ever known. He was the top executive of one of the nation's largest business enterprises. His leadership carried weight not alone in business and industry at home and across the seas, but he was also a success in his home with his family, in his community and in his church. His was one of the most remarkably well-balanced lives that I have ever known. I thought it interesting then that in his own, his wife's and his children's appraisal he would have been equally and more happily a success had he been less "successful" dollar-and-position-wise in industry and enabled to live not only longer (for he died at 56) but also with greater satisfactions in less strenuously pressured days.

I think now of another man whom I place high on the list of those I would nominate as successes. His work holds little glamour. He is on a modest salary in personal service to another. He has perhaps never had his picture in the newspaper. It is quite likely that he would not be included on a list of the "ten best" of anything—that is—in man's book. In God's it is, I am sure, quite different. This man has one of the finest, warmest, and most radiant Christian families that I know. The children have married and established fine homes. Both parents have served loyally in church and community. When I see these neatly dressed and amiable parents enter the church to worship, I am looking at truly successful people. When I look at the children, the proof spills over.

Our age is desperately in need of making some important reappraisals in life values. Linked with many other offenders, irresponsible advertising has created new definitions of success, prestige and value until we are branded as having "arrived" only if a certain car is at our door, a certain whiskey is on our shelf, a certain club lists our name on its roster.

"He has showed you, O Man, what is good; and what does the Lord require of you but to do justice and to love kindness, and to walk humbly with your God?"

For A Wide, Wide World

It WAS EARLY morning. I was crossing Nicollet Avenue on Franklin in the city of Minneapolis when I saw the boys. There were two of them about fourteen years old waiting for a traffic light to change. "We have been getting too cityfied" they may have been thinking, for they had knapsacks on their backs and were headed for open country and the wide, wide world.

More than one of us can recall some years long past when other boys with knapsacks headed adventurously into the world beyond the city limits. It is a "wide, wide world," however familiar the numerous corners of it become. Even the television program by that name reflects the awe with which adults and youth alike approach this world of ours.

What a fascinating experience it would be to ride Sputnik! Circling the world at the rate of 18,000 miles an hour, Sputnik looks down on millions of amazing scenes and contrasting peoples—from a Manhattan penthouse to a Pacific atoll. Down below, Turkey and Syria seethe with tension; Little Rock and other cities know a smouldering bitterness; Central America watches political cauldrons boil; Asia debates within herself which world power to follow; Russia presses on relentlessly in search of new status and influence. What Sputnik could see if it had the eyes of man is not a pretty picture. Heartache and tension, fear and frustration,

pride and greed "walk through the earth," to use a Psalmist's
phrase.

There are many more pleasant things that we could think
about. We could point out paragraph by paragraph and chapter after chapter the remarkable achievements of men. What
a thrilling story! But however long a time we might spend
reviewing all these accomplishments we would still be confronted with the realization that only the wearing of rose-
colored glasses will make it possible for any of us to believe
that the world is anything but sick.

The Lord described the world of Isaiah's day, and I am
afraid the world of our day, too, when He said: "The whole
head is sick, and the whole heart faint. From the sole of the
foot even to the head there is no soundness in it, but bruises
and sores and bleeding wounds; they are not pressed out, or
bound up, or softened with oil." Isaiah then continues, "If
the Lord of hosts had not left us a few survivors, we should
have been like Sodom, and become like Gomorrah . . . Hear
the word of the Lord . . . Give ear to the teaching of our God."

The Lord has spoken again and again to the world spiritually ill. The present day symptoms of world sickness may
involve new names and new places with some apparently new
forms of treatment for apparently new diseases; but there is
little new under the sun in sin and nothing new under the sun
in treatment since the day of our Savior's coming.

Carved into the pulpit of Central Lutheran Church are
words which tell the unending task which is the Church's in
our wide and soul-sick world. The words are these, "Go ye
into all the world and preach the Gospel to every creature."
The Apostle Mark in his recording of these words added
these, "He that believes and is baptized will be saved; but he
who does not believe will be condemned."

Sputnik may circle the globe and with unseeing eyes look down on a people vastly superior to their forebears in scientific knowledge, in humanitarian efforts, in skills and abilities. But if Sputnik had eyes to truly see and ears to really hear, Sputnik would have to record for the records that in the mid-Twentieth Century man still needs saving from himself and his sin. But Sputnik would also have to record that redeemed man is the most privileged ever to have lived in this wide, wide world.

Then Sings My Soul

COINCIDENTAL with another assignment in New York City and through the gracious arrangements made by another, I attended a breakfast meeting in the great Sheraton-Astor Hotel ballroom on Times Square. It was an unusual breakfast. More than twenty-five hundred men were present at that early hour. The occasion was a review of the Madison Square Garden campaign conducted under the leadership of Billy Graham. It was also a meeting preliminary to a vast doorbell-ringing visitation of Greater New York by thousands of church members from more than a thousand churches.

One highlight of that morning was the dynamic singing by this assembly of men. The song leader was Beverly Shea. His captivating voice led with these words, "Then sings my soul my Savior God to Thee, how *great* Thou art, how *great* Thou art . . ."

I have another music memory that traces back to a college choir experience. Here, too, the memory relates to words which repeated themselves in a particular number—words that can well stand repeating . . . "For He is a *great* God, for He is a *great* God . . ."

How often we have subtly, unconsciously, ridiculously leveled God down to the mere measure of superhuman nature and capability and in our minds have stripped from Him the glory, the wisdom, the power and might that is His. Several things have occurred in our religious life as a result.

We have lost some of the thrill of our faith. Have you ever stood amidst the clouds on a high mountain peak and with a sense of awe and wonder watched the warm sunlight give way to huge snowflakes in a drifting cloud and then in moments return again? Across the miles a glacier slips its way imperceptibly down the side of another great peak. All of this by God's creative power. "How great Thou art. . . ."

Have you stood over a surgical table in a hospital watching the skilled fingers of the surgeon probe their way as though with eyes of their own through the maze of muscles, tendons, veins, arteries, organs and all that composes a human body? Have you wondered at the instantaneous reverse action of your hand placed carelessly on a hot stove, at the lightning-quick flick of an eyelid closing the gate against a whirling particle of dust? Again, all of this by God's creative power. "How great Thou art, how great Thou art. . . ."

But more remarkable by far than the beauties of a sinking sun, the sparkle of a dewdrop on a knife-like blade of grass; more awesome than the determined movement of a tide; more thrilling than the delicateness of a baby's ear is the wonder of God's touch upon a human soul. "How great Thou art. . . ."

Have you sat with an elderly lady crippled up with arthritis, alone in the outliving of her family, yet radiantly beautiful in spite of facial crevasses of age and strong of heart and spirit however stooped her shoulders with her years? "How great Thou art. . . ."

Have you chatted with a sparkling young couple effervescent in their love, eager in their yearning for the years of togetherness, whose lives are individually witness to the power of Christ to make clean-cut and beautiful souls? "How great Thou art. . . ."

Have you stood toe to toe with a rugged man his face still scarred a bit with past years' evidence of dissipated life yet scarcely seen or noted in the overwhelming strength and calmness of new faith and life. ". . . you were washed, you were sanctified, you were justified in the name of our Lord Jesus Christ and in the Spirit of our God." "How great Thou art. . . ."

". . . then sings my soul my *Savior* God to Thee," for great as Thou art, Creator of the universe and man—Thou art seen as greater still in the wonder of Thy power to save.

"Play It"

EACH OF US knows of days and even hours when we are more spiritually perceptive than normally. Such an hour for me was one spent at a concert by the Minneapolis Symphony. The sensitive musicianship of the orchestra was an inspiration. The superb direction of its conductor, Antal Dorati, intrigued me. But it was in the compositions themselves, expressive of the mood and message of the composer, that I was reminded of this thought. Dr. Harry Emerson Fosdick had penned it. He wrote, "We defend religion too much. Vital religion, like good music, needs no defense but rendition. A wrangling controversy in support of religion is precisely as if the members of an orchestra would beat folks over their heads with their violins to prove that music is beautiful. But such procedure is no way to prove that music is beautiful. Rather play it!"

Christianity is rarely either defended or proved effectively through logic and debate. This does not mean that Christianity has no defense and cannot stand careful scrutiny. However, adherents to the faith are commonly won first through the attractive witness of lives in which the Christian faith is vital. When Christian lives are like that, then Christian truth gains a sympathetic hearing. In evident contrast, a sympathetic hearing is often lost when professors of the faith are unattractive witnesses to it.

Nothing, of course, is more important than the message of the Savior Christ. It is interesting to note, however, that it was said of early followers of Christ that it could be seen that they "had been with Jesus." They were more than carriers of information. They were more than drab covers on a stimulating book. They were actually a part of the story — "samples," if you please, of the power of Christ at work in human lives.

"See how they love one another" was another of the conclusions drawn by those who stood on the outside looking in. Few things will create as great interest and curiosity as this.

Mr. Brown is a homeowner with a new neighbor. Their first contact was not a pleasant one. By way of introduction the neighbor said, "Hello, sir, I'm your new neighbor. I've bought the property next door." "Hello, yourself," was the reply. "You may have bought the property, but you also bought yourself a lawsuit. Your fence is two feet over on my property," said Mr. Brown. "Well, I'm sorry for that inconvenience to you," said the new neighbor. "I guess I'll have to do some fence moving very shortly." It was with some surprise that Mr. Brown heard this. That fence had been a real issue with the former owner whose stubborn anger had flamed a dozen times on the subject. It was then that Mr. Brown settled the issue by saying, "Well, if that is the way you feel about it, why don't we just forget the whole thing? It doesn't really matter."

The Christian life is more than a dressing-up of everyday life with a veneer of partial reverence and by occasional expression in pious terminology. If we would prove our faith, we must "play it," for "faith without works is dead" . . . "but the fruit of the Spirit is love, joy, peace, long-suffering, gentleness, goodness, faith, meekness, temperance. . . ."

Stop With A Star

THE TALE has been told and retold perhaps half a hundred ways. With at least some resemblance to the way James Truslow Adams told it, we tell again that provocative bit of philosophy from the Amazon region of South America. Native burden bearers had disappointed their white masters on a safari. With some disgust the party leader returned over the jungle path to find the natives resting in the cool grasses. With explosive anger he scolded them for their incompetence and laziness. The excuse given by the native leader was: "We had to stop long enough for our souls to catch up to our bodies."

Life takes on many peculiar dimensions for all of us. Sometimes life seems all pressed in upon us as though the past were present and the future present as well. Time simply stands still. It hangs heavily like a high-humidity day.

Or there are times when life becomes a rather breathless experience. It handles you like a dusty southwest whirlpool of air that picks you up and sets you down, picks you up and sets you down again. Breathlessly you are being moved across the landscape of life. Much of the experience is exciting. Some of it is downright thrilling. Part of it feels as though you have stepped on to the first step of a high-speed escalator and there is no choice left but to keep on your way. How nice!—if only you could stop or even slow down long enough to get a revitalized soul back into a somewhat rested body capable of housing it.

How does it work for you? Do you ever snap a bit when replying to a normally intelligent (or unintelligent) request? Don't you want to be bothered? Is the telephone your avowed enemy? The mail a conspirator against your peace of mind? Are your children terribly noisy "all the time"? Do your friends and associates lack understanding and appreciation of "busy you"? Friend, if this pictures you, chances are your body has run away from your soul.

Martha was such a hostess one day when Jesus was her guest. "But he is Mary's guest, too," she thought as she grew hotter and more miserable over the dinner stove while Mary was visiting with Jesus—completely rapt in her attention to Him. Finally, when Martha could contain her fenced-in temper no longer, she burst into the conversation to express what she had on her mind. Jesus' reply went something like this: "Martha, you are a nice person and unusually efficient. There are not many like you in the world. You are one of my best friends, as are Mary and Lazarus. But, Martha, you do get desperately excited and concerned about some things that may not be quite as important as you make them out to be. . . . One thing is needful. Mary hath chosen that good portion, which shall not be taken away from her."

There are various qualities in life each of which has its unique value and makes its singular contribution. One of these less honored than most in our jet age is the quiet calm pursuit of spiritual life and depth and strength and growth with Him Who is the source of Life.

If ye would hasten fast and far, Stop with a star.
    Stop with the Star of Bethlehem, the Christ.
And in that hour of silence be renewed to live
    In palace gates or coach-house, work or play—
        Strong man of God, strong man of God.

I Know

"ONE TEST is worth a thousand expert opinions." This was the catchy slogan which I saw in a St. Paul testing laboratory more than twenty years ago. I have never forgotten it. I suppose the truth of this statement has been verified millions of times in scores of fields even beyond the walls of science and laboratory rooms. We want to *know*. We want to be sure.

"Sputnik" and "Muttnik," Russia's introductory presentation to space travel, suggest some interesting "speculations" in the realm of our knowledge. Drop into the past by some fifty-odd years and seat yourself at a crossroads grocery cracker barrel. Shift the conversation around to possible future space travel or even to the now-conventional turbo-prop or jet-transport travel coast to coast. Listen to the raucous laughter as you predict such feats within a span of fifty years, when in that hour even the automobile is only a wildman's dream. "I *know* we can," says one. "I *know* we can't" is the reply of another.

What *can* a man know that will hold fast for him? On what can a man depend? The French built an impregnable Maginot line only to have it penetrated by the Germans a few years later. The submarine was built to destroy world navies but it did not. The airplane was certain to force wars to cease but did not. The atom bomb should frighten people into genuinely peaceful relationship together—but it will not. Thus we have spoken of atom and molecule, matter and man, and have said, "I know," "I know," "I know" . . .

Is there some *one* thing we may know and be assured of which will hold its truth and force for today and tomorrow and the day after tomorrow? There is! And it is to be found in the Christian faith where a man can say "I know"—and have it hold.

Generations ago in the days when Jesus walked this earth a young man blind from the day of his birth was given his sight by the Master. As astonishing as the event was in that community, there were those who challenged the truth of this miracle, seeking their best to discredit the Christ. The target of attack was the young man, whom they sought their best to confuse. Who He was? What He did? When He did it? What happened?—all of these were questions for the young man's weary ears. It was finally in desperation and disgust that the young man turned to his tormenting challengers with the words . . . "whether He (that is Christ) is a sinner, I do not know; *one thing I know,* that though I was blind, now I see."

Jesus Christ is One who has made it possible in an ever-changing world for man to say of one thing, "I know." That "one thing" is of eternal significance, but of lifetime significance as well. It has to do with a man's faith. It has to do with his future. It has to do with a man's soul. And nowhere does man have such critical need for assurance, as in the matters of his soul.

Blind in sin, man finds spiritual sight in the healing power of Christ. The empty cross and the open tomb are forever symbols of this power. But does God mean this for me? I cannot answer for all the mysteries of His nature. I cannot logically explain a love like Christ's for me. I cannot dissect, bisect, trisect faith and hope and love and prove by graphs and formulas and geometric circles who God is and how He loves me.

But He does. And I can see it in the stars and in a song. I can see it in the lily by the gate, in the sparrow in her flight. I can see it in the struggle of a man to understand and love his brother. But I can see it best at a cross outside a city wall; at a garden with its empty tomb. And I can hear it when He says, "He that has the Son has life." Then I can say "I know, I know what most I need to know until that day when all things strange will disappear and we shall know Him evermore."

Just Living

LITTLE WILLIE had an interesting answer for his mother. She had been quite concerned over the silence in his room and felt sure that he was up to some mischief. She called out, "Willie, what are you doing?" His reply had a bit of the impatience in it when he said, "Can't you see, Mother, that I'm just living?"

A lot of folks on this Christmas holiday have been "just living." Perhaps the sudden shifting of gears away from hectic "normal" days has had a bit of awesome silence in it. Isolated for the moment away from the routine of making a living, you have used the day as a wonderful opportunity to spend time with family and friends. But perhaps you have also done a bit of serious thinking,—about some of the wonderful things that are a part of Christmas.

Something wonderful? There was the United Press story out of Munich, Germany, about airlift crews that gave up their Christmas holiday for the refugees. There was the story from Associated Press telling of the suburban Oak Park wife and her children who, abandoned by the husband and father, were given the merriest of days—groceries, a Christmas tree and all the trimmings—by the police who found them.

On other continents the great refugee flood sweeps across the lands and reminds us of the kind of world in which we live. Millions of dispossessed and homeless people are looking for a place to hang their thin and tattered hats.

Christmas day finds itself in a peculiar setting of contrasts, does it not? I am reminded of something Ralph Waldo Emerson once told when as a young minister he attended a Bible Society convention in a southern state. By mere chance the meetings were held in a room the windows of which opened on a slave market where Negroes were being auctioned off. So Emerson described the scene, "one ear, therefore, heard the glad tidings of great joy while the other was regaled with, 'Going, gentlemen, going, going, gone.'" Then he added, "Almost without changing our position we might aid in sending Scriptures into Africa or bid for four children that had been kidnapped in Africa."

It is such an intolerable contradiction that we also face in our generation where we may listen with one ear to faith, hope and charity in the Christian Gospel and with the other to encouragement toward war, brutality and violence. It is unhappily true that even in our own America we are often socially as well as spiritually asleep. We as a nation have acquired a great deal of education and polish. Many sit quite comfortably and deeply cushioned in ease and high prosperity. We find our powers of industry and finance the envy of much of the world. But, and this is immeasurably important, we have often weakened rather than strengthened our moral and spiritual steering wheels. And great power under the hood is risky business if the steering column is frail.

The message of Christmas is more than vague generalities about "peace on earth, good will to men." Though perhaps

an attempt to define that phrase might result in a million in-
nocuous answers, the sum total of Christmas and its story is
not vague nor is it confusing. It is quite simply that God came
down to sinful man in the person of His Son, the Saviour
Christ. It is in this Christ that men shall find their deepest
needs met, their fondest hopes realized. In Him men may
know the secret of more than "just living."

Can You Say
The Lord's Prayer?

MEN AND WOMEN all over America not only held their breaths but joined their prayers with those of the parents, neighbors, friends, the police and scores of others seeking to bring Benny Hooper back to the surface alive from the deep well into which he had fallen. America was waiting. But hope was running out when the courageous Negro, Woodson, tugged at the arm of little Benny, heard a groan, and said, "Then I talked to God." "It's a miracle! It is a miracle!" was the expression of many. Little Benny had been brought up from an almost certain death. Today, apart from the special attention he received, he is a normal boy again.

I am sure that there were a great number of prayers that were prayed, many of them most sincerely asking that God by His intervening power would make the rescue efforts successful. The prayers were answered.

Have you ever been puzzled about the use of prayer,— the thrilling answers, the seeming denials? The problem is never one of the power of God. It may, however, lie in us in areas we have not understood.

Someone has made this rather helpful analysis. It came to me from some radio-listener friends in the Minnesota State Prison Alcoholics Anonymous group. It begins with a question: CAN I SAY THE LORD'S PRAYER?

I cannot say "Our" if I live in a water-tight spiritual compartment; if I think a special place in heaven is reserved just for my own little group.

I cannot say "Father" if I do not believe that He is actually my spiritual father.

I cannot say "who art in heaven" if I do not believe in a hereafter.

I cannot say "hallowed by Thy name" if I, who am called by His name, do not want myself to be holy.

I cannot say "Thy kingdom come" if I am so occupied with earthly things that I am laying up no treasure in His kingdom.

I cannot say "Thy will be done" if I am questioning, resentful or disobedient to His will for me.

I cannot say "on earth as it is in heaven" if I am not prepared to devote my life here to His service.

I cannot say "Give us this day our daily bread" if I am only asking Him to erase my past mistakes and do not ask for strength and guidance just for today.

I cannot say "Forgive us our trespasses as we forgive those who trespass against us" if I harbor a grudge against anyone.

I cannot say "Lead us not into temptation" if I deliberately place myself or remain in a position where I am likely to be tempted.

I cannot say "Deliver us from evil" if I am not prepared to fight in the spiritual realm with a weapon of prayer.

I cannot say "Thine is the kingdom" if I do not accord the King the disciplined obedience of a loyal subject.

I cannot say "Thine is the power" if I fear what men may do or what my neighbors may think.

I cannot say "Thine is the glory?" if I am seeking glory for myself.

For me it is a thrilling thing to discover the understanding of prayer that has come to some of my friends in the A.A. group. Prayer has become a natural and indispensable part of their daily lives, but not as a superstitious, "rabbit-foot" type of wishfulness.

My friend John is an unusual man. For a long time he was an unusually hopeless man. By his own claim he was as pathetic a case of alcoholism as is possible this side of death. He appraised his past most graphically by saying that the Lillian Roth story was "Sunday School" by comparison. The price paid by his wife, his children and others close to him was more than human endurance could normally take. Then came the change, a "conversion" in its most dramatic sense. For a time God linked a friend to the side of John for 24 hours a day who helped him live and think and breathe and judge. But the secret of secrets for John lay in that he never took his head off the pillow in the morning without acknowledging to God his utter helplessness to win the day alone and without claiming the power of God to supplant his weakness.

John is an unusual man. He is now unusually successful. He has a beautiful home. He owns two cars. His family is radiantly happy. John is a miracle of God come from out of a deeper pit than Benny Hooper. However weak in himself, he has become a strong man of God. John has learned some secrets in how to pray.

Seek Ye First The Kingdom

THE LEGISLATURE has come to a close and has concluded those hectic hours of wrestling with the dollars and cents
expenditures that are necessary in order to do the work
required within this state of ours. Thinking about dollars and
cents that we spend as a state or as a nation carried my
thoughts to a column "Strictly Personal" written by Sidney J.
Harris for the CHICAGO DAILY NEWS. The column carried
some uncomfortable notes on our high standard of living.

Do you know:

That crime and delinquency cost more than six times the
entire cost of all public education in the United States?

That for each dollar spent for schools we spend two dollars and ninety-six cents for military purposes, a dollar and
sixty cents for new automobiles, and a dollar and seventy-five
cents for amusement?

That we spend more money for comic books than for all
the text books used in our elementary and high schools?

That although research can help conquer blindness, only
about three million dollars a year is spent on eye research,
but twelve million dollars a year is spent on unprescribed
eye lotions, washes, mascaras, eyebrow pencil and eye
shadow?

That last year Americans spent a staggering one and a half billion dollars on travel abroad but the nation spent only a paltry ten million dollars on mental health research, which is one of the most pressing and widespread medical problems of our time?

That, according to the American Heart Association, only twenty-five million dollars went into heart research last year which is less than the nation spent for buying decks of playing cards?

That in our country today there are some three million excessive drinkers and seven hundred and fifty thousand alcoholics which are more than all the polio, cancer and TB cases put together, yet we spent two hundred million dollars on the prevention of cancer and TB while the American public spent more than nine billion dollars on alcohol?

That each year we spend about two and a half billion dollars in hospitals but nearly twice as much for tobacco?

That though some people think that some doctors' fees are high, the nation's total medical bill is only one-third as much as the nation spends for alcoholic drinks?

That some think that drug bills may be high, but we spend a billion dollars a year more for items involved in personal care such as hair lotions and toilet waters?

We perhaps have no right to speak glowingly about our high standard of living until we are able to spend our money as wisely as we are able to make it. The ultimate test of a civilization is not its power or its riches but its sense of value. Every flourishing empire of the past collapsed because it began paying more attention to the incidentals than to the essentials of a good life.

It reminds me of what someone some time ago suggested, that too often we are majoring in minors; or you might reverse that and say minoring in majors as well. Such figures and facts bring us back to this whole question of what really counts in life. We are brought back to realize that *real* answers have to do with human personality, human welfare, the eternal spirit which God has given to any man; and that if we miss out on the great prescription which the Lord Himself gave, we will have ultimately missed out on living.

"Is not life more than food and the body more than clothing? . . . But seek first his kingdom and his righteousness, and all these things shall be yours as well."

Do You Really ..?

IT WAS LATE at night. Ordinarily it would not have been a pleasant drive. Rain was plastering the windshield. The wipers joined in a frantic though rhythmical beat. But we were comfortable, enjoying our conversation together; and I for one was not eager to have it end.

My guest was the noted economic consultant, lecturer, church leader and splendid Christian personality, Dr. Alfred P. Haake of Park Ridge, Illinois. We spoke of many things but principally of the Christian Church, those who compose it and their responsibility to it in the modern community. It was then that Dr. Haake told of an incident in Detroit when he had been given the opportunity to speak before a group of Protestant clergymen. In his address he made the following statement: "I think that one of our troubles in the Christian Church is that too many of us, and too many of you, do not *really* believe in God." There was immediate reaction as would be expected. One of the clergymen arose, challenged Dr. Haake's statement and requested an explanation.

The reply which Dr. Haake gave took this turn. "It seems apparent," he said, "that the Christian Church as God's instrument in the world is not all that God intended it to be. We have often failed both God and our fellow men. Perhaps it is that we don't really believe what we claim about the power of God." He then asked, "Do you really believe in God when you, as pastors, step into the pulpit to preach? Do you really believe that the Holy Spirit will work through the preaching of the Word of God as promised and will actually accomplish some miracles? Do you believe that it can take hold of the alcoholic in the back pew and open up to him a new life? Do you believe that the Gospel conveys a power to reach and change the life of a young couple seated side by side in the pew but who are miles apart in their marriage and are ready for divorce? Do you really believe in God?"

"But," said Dr. Haake, as we continued our visit in the night, "I went on to add something else. I was not alone challenging the pastor in his pulpit. I was also challenging myself and my fellow laymen. Here I had these questions to ask. Do we really believe in God and prove it by our relationships? Do we really believe in God when it comes to relating our faith to our homes, our businesses, our abilities, our contacts with those around us? Do we really believe in God and prove it when it comes to our pocket-book declaration of faith? Do we trust God? Do we take Him seriously? Or do we dabble a little with religious window-dressing?"

It is now almost ten years since our conversation that night when we drove through the rain but those questions are as fresh to my mind as yesterday. For we must ask such questions. The answers will vary. Some answers will be excitingly positive. Some will be depressingly negative.

Is my own personal world different because I believe?
Is the world about me different because I believe?
Is my church different because I believe?
Do I really believe? . . .
Perhaps I have just been saying so.

> "Be exalted, O God, above the Heavens!
> Let Thy glory be over all the earth!"

Take A Second Look

IN YEARS GONE BY, Cedric Adams, the news announcer and columnist, would occasionally carry a column paragraph entitled, "Thoughts While Shaving." He, like a great many others, discovered that some of his most creative thinking took place during the performance of that mundane chore. A much less mundane chore for me has been that of getting my haircuts and this, I suspect, is true for two reasons. The first is that my barber, Len, does an unusually fine job of cutting my hair. The second reason is that he usually shares with me some of the things that he has been hearing and thinking about. One day he told this story.

A medical doctor had developed a successful practice which resulted in its being very demanding of his time and energy. The pressures of his work left him little time for his home and family. He came and went with only superficial contacts and in a period of time a subtle estrangement developed. He noted among other traits that his wife had become edgy and moody. Visiting one day with a doctor friend he quite unkindly referred to his wife as "the battle axe." Fortunately for him, his friend was no novice and had learned a few lessons himself in the department of family relations. He suggested, "Maybe the trouble isn't with your wife at all. Perhaps the real trouble is with you and you cannot see it. Why don't you surprise her with some beautiful roses today, express a word of appreciation for what she is and does and then see what happens? Go out of your way for her for a change."

It was a thoughtful doctor who stopped at the florist for roses that day. He brought them home, presented them to his startled wife and half mumbled a few gracious words, his complexion a bit pink in obvious embarrassment. She thanked him graciously, got a vase from the corner cupboard, watered the flowers and then returned to the kitchen to finish preparation for dinner. It was a strange sound that the doctor heard as he sat down with his newspaper; his wife was humming cheerfully in the kitchen. It had been a long time since he had heard that.

Now another voice was heard. His little boy had entered the kitchen from a side door. He chattered with his mother and entered the living room to look at the flowers his mother had told him about. Then, bubbling over, he said, "Daddy, I guess you do really love us, don't you? You wouldn't bring us flowers if you didn't, would you?"

The youngster ran on out to play and the daddy returned to his paper. But he wasn't reading it. He couldn't. The print was blurred, for his eyes were misty. What a fool he had been! How critical he had been of his wife, how impatient with her edginess. How he had starved her and his son, too. The fine home and the quality groceries for the table were no substitute for affection, understanding and his own self-giving. He had thought the problem rested quite simply in his wife's irritable disposition, her unexplainable dissatisfactions in spite of everything a homemaker could ask for. Now he had found the answer. "Things" are only substitutes for real "life-togetherness." She had really been quite reasonable about the schedule peculiarities, quite well adjusted to the concessions to be made to others and their needs. But she had needed him and the knowledge of his love as he, too, had needed her and had not been aware 'till now.

"The eye of the understanding is like the eye of the sense, for as you may see great objects through small crannies or holes, so you may see great axioms of nature through small and contemptible instances." — Bacon.

Oh, What
A Beautiful World!

"OH, WHAT A beautiful morning! Oh, what a beautiful day!" It must have been under the spell of beautiful spring days that Richard Rodgers and Oscar Hammerstein were moved to such lilting lyrics as these. My neighbors are moved, too. When I pulled into the driveway today, I found them leaning over the back fence, intent on nothing more than to bask in the wonder of today.

I have been flying today—and the world is fully as beautiful from up in space. I am still under the spell of the beauty of the earth beneath as it rolled under me in panoramic view—the patchwork quilt of green—all shades—as one farm community blended into another in a kaleidoscopic array of earth-colored patches.

There was another beautiful sight from our plane windows, too. Off to our right a few thousand feet we saw a long drawn-out tear drop hanging in the sky, making a slow descent toward earth. Our pilot drew our attention to it and reminded us that today's balloon flight was to set another record of man's flight into the stratosphere. Why? That the genius of man at work in the world of technology, with the rapid accumulation of fantastic knowledge of the universe in which he lives, might make this world an even more wondrous place in which to live.

And it is not that *man* is creating all this, whether it be radar, the power wrapped in the nucleus of the atom, the different waves in the air that bring either sound or picture into the home. It is that God has created this fantastic world! It is only needed for man to give himself to the unfolding of these mysteries of the universe. Radar has always been at hand—the unwelcome flying bat has had it built into his system for countless ages as a protective device. The power at the heart of the atom has always been locked within it. The sound waves, the picture waves—these have always surrounded us. Man has only needed to break open these mysteries and to learn how to harness them for the well-being and the comfort of man. Oh, what a wonderful world!

Do you know that today's gorgeous sunshine would have cost the governments of the earth more than a hundred million times a million dollars for twelve hours of its heat and light and energy? That if our federal government were to have to pay for sunlight for the continental United States alone, it would call for an annual budget of 686 trillion dollars, says Harlan Truman. Is this not a remarkable world? If only man could harness such a tremendous source of energy!

A tree can. Each leaf is an engine, a factory within itself which is being run from the dynamo, the sun, ninety-three million miles away. What manufacturer, what scientist, would not give his right arm to know how to harness such power, and without one cent of "overhead"! All during the day the leaf is absorbing the energy of the sun to run its starch factory; at night, by some secret conversion process, it converts from a starch to a sugar plant, shooting its sap down twigs and branches and trunk to furnish growing materials. The catalyst is chlorophyll—the only thing on earth with

power to trap the energy of the sun to use for the manu-
facture of foods. On this green chlorophyll all animal life
depends. What a great, wide, beautiful, wonderful world!

> "The heavens are telling the glory of God; and the
>   firmament proclaims his handiwork.
> Day to day pours forth speech, and night to night
>   declares his knowledge.
> There is no speech, nor are there words;
>   their voice is not heard;
> Yet their voice goes out through all the earth,
>   and their words to the end of the world."

Nevertheless

I FOUND A little flyer on the counter at a bakery one day, free for the customer's taking. On the front was a picture which showed a man standing on the rail of a bridge, his coat and hat lying over the rail, his hands clasped together, his body poised to jump into the river. The caption at the top of the picture said, "So You Think You Have Had Tough Breaks." The story inside went something like this:

When you don't get the breaks and the defeats pile up; when you're discouraged and don't care about the future; when you're ready to toss in the sponge and quit;—take a minute to consider this man's record. Failed in business 1831; defeated for legislature 1832; failed in business again 1833; elected to legislature 1834; sweetheart died 1835; nervous breakdown 1836; defeated for Speaker 1838; defeated for land officer 1843; defeated for Congress 1843; elected to Congress 1846; defeated for re-election 1848; defeated for senate 1855; defeated for Vice-president 1856; defeated for senate 1858; elected President of the United States 1860. Who was he? An obscure country boy without any education who refused to let it handicap him. He refused to remain obscure. He refused to stay uneducated; he educated himself. He refused to plead hard luck. He refused to accept failure. He refused to turn back when all the odds seemed hopeless. He believed in and practiced simplicity, honesty, industry, persistence, tolerance, friendliness and faith. He was Abraham Lincoln.

One of the remarkable things about life is that though it so often appears that our unhappy destiny is sealed, there are alternatives in charting our lives. Many, of course, do not accept these alternate patterns of life. Lincoln did. Others have done so as well.

In the story of St. Luke we find that certain Pharisees came to warn Jesus of the danger of death from Herod. Christ is able to see the possibility of a swift ending to his life, but his reply to the Pharisees is a quick, sharp, decisive retort. "Go and tell that fox, 'Behold I cast out demons and perform cures today and tomorrow, and the third day finish the course. *Nevertheless*, I must go my way today and to-morrow and the day following.'" *Nevertheless!*

We need not look alone to the "name" personalities of history in order to find a spirit of "nevertheless." You know them as well as I. You may, in fact, be one.

There is the widow whose husband died when her five children were little tots, the oldest one eight years old. There was no insurance to draw on. The pension was so meager as to buy groceries for only half of the family. Nevertheless this courageous mother made a way as home-maker, mother, schoolteacher, county superintendent. There was sewing and patching, scrubbing and dusting, advising and disciplining, skimping and making-do, in order that the children might be given educations to fit themselves for service to society. *Nevertheless!*

There is the paralytic consigned by others to a life of being waited on, all possible personal maintenance or useful service to others but a dream. *Nevertheless*, with partial retraining of his limbs and the genius of an agile mind, he has made himself the most valuable worker in a company where he has designed new machines and developed new methods. *Nevertheless!*

There is the former alcoholic destined by most who knew his story to end his days as he had lived them, a human derelict. *Nevertheless,* claiming the promises of God, clinging to a friend, and determined to win a new world, he astonished his counsellors with a buoyant sobriety, a new career and an active participation in his church and community.

"Nevertheless" stories, at their remarkable best, are the stories of men and women who, against odds commonly accepted as impossible, have gone on to achievement and victory. You will find exceptions to the rule but in the main the secret will be found to lie in promises like these: "Be strong in the Lord and in the strength of His might," "We know that in everything God works for good with those who love him," and "With God all things are possible." "*Nevertheless . . .*"

"Wrong On The Inside"

THIS IS THE confession of a famous radio commentator and philosopher made publicly to his vast network audience.

The commentator had been invited to Hollywood for the production of a biographical movie short depicting his unusually successful career. Filming had been completed and the "rushes" were to be viewed with the producer, the director, the commentator and others in attendance. The lights were dimmed and the story was flashed on the screen.

Only minutes had passed when a voice in the room called out, "Turn it off! Turn it off!" The projector was turned off, the studio lights were turned on and some astonished people looked about them to determine who it was that had given the order. It was the radio commentator. He pointed toward the screen and then asked what seemed to be a totally incongruous question: "Who is that?"

Following a moment of stunned silence, they replied, "Why, that is a picture of you."

He asked another question, "Do you mean that the man pictured on the screen with his jowls hanging to his collarbone, with the deep hard lines etched in his face, with scarcely a visible hair on his head is me? If that is true, I don't want you to ever show this picture to a living soul!"

When the radio commentator had told this true story from out of his personal experience, he went on to add these comments. "Somehow, without being aware of it, I had come to think of myself in terms quite at odds with the truth. I had foolishly believed that when I walked into a room well filled with ladies their hearts began to beat a bit faster because I was present. For many years I had looked at myself through rose-colored glasses and thought what I wanted to think. The embarrassing experience in that studio was the harshest one of my life, but it was also one most worthwhile." He then concluded, "And what do you see when you look at yourself, that which you want to see, or that which others see and live with?"

It is true that most of us look at ourselves with tinted glasses,—tinted, that is, to place us in the light in which we want to see ourselves, but which may be very unrealistic.

Physical characteristics are obviously not of prime importance. Some of the world's most valuable personalities had little to commend them in "good looks" as witness a Lincoln or, by Scriptural admission, Christ Himself. But what do we look like in personality and spirit to others? What of our kindness or lack of it; our selflessness or selfishness; our humility or pride; our cheerfulness or gloominess? What of all the attributes which make us either negative or positive personalities in human society or to God?

Mr. Lincoln during the Civil War stepped out of a hospital room into the corridor only to move inadvertently into the path of a young man who was hurrying by. They collided. The young man angrily spoke up without looking to see to whom it was he was addressing his words. He said, "What's the matter with you? Can't you look out for a young gentleman?"

Abraham Lincoln's reply was as soft-spoken as were his

eyes but, touching his breast, he asked, "Young man, what's wrong with you on the inside?"

Mr. Lincoln was well aware that we are prone to stumbling in our human relationships when there is something "wrong on the inside."

Jesus Christ came to right that which is "wrong on the inside." He made this clear to the well educated, highly religious, well-to-do Nicodemus who with a disturbed heart thought the answer lay in self-renovation. Jesus said, "You must be born again,"—you need a new heart. By the Spirit of God new hearts *are* born and even the angels rejoice.

One Thing

JUST "ONE THING" can make all the difference. It did for those aboard a streamlined train in the East. It was speeding through the night with no apparent danger to mar its rhythmical click. But the rhythm was suddenly broken. A "hot box" developed in an axle housing of just one of the dozens of wheels. The wheel locked and the car jumped the track dragging other cars with it. A rare but major railroad catastrophe took place. A score of lives were lost because of just "one thing."

It takes no more than one thing to alter human events beyond the expected. *One* bent tooth in the tiniest gear of a watch can render the watch useless. *One* tire blown out at high speed can hurtle a car from the road. *One* grade point can make the difference between a high honor and no honor, between passing and failing.

Just "one thing" can also make a difference in a man's spiritual world as well. It may make the difference between a self-life and a Christ-life, between a futile life and an abundant life. This was true for an attractive young man whose story is recounted by St. Mark.

He must have been an unusually splendid young man. It is evident that he was a leader in the community. He had a fine education. He came from one of the so-called "better

families." In addition, he was successful and financially
well-fixed. Picture him one day standing on the fringe of a
small but intent crowd listening to a new teacher. The stranger's name is Jesus. He speaks of God the heavenly Father and
of man and his need for a right relationship to Him. He
speaks of a man's soul as being estranged, disturbed and
frustrated—out-of-tune with God.

Our young listener is intrigued by what he hears. For
the first time someone is speaking to his deepest needs. He
returns to his home but to an unusually restless evening. His
appetite is gone. Reading is a bore; the scroll is a blur. Nor
does sleep come easily. What a disturbing personality the
rich young ruler has found in this man Jesus. One might be
pleased by Him or angered by Him but one can scarcely
ignore Him. It is as though one's whole soul is laid bare
before His warm but penetrating eyes.

It is early the next morning when the rich young ruler
hurries down to the village market with an almost breathless
hope of finding Jesus. He must have a question answered.
But Jesus and His followers are already on their way toward
the next village. This must not be. The young ruler must not
lose Him. Hurrying down the dusty road, all dignity and
poise shed like his fallen silk cloak, he slips to his knees at
the feet of the rugged, sun-bronzed Jesus and blurts out his
disturbing and long-repressed question: "Good Teacher,
what must I do to inherit eternal life?"

At first it must have seemed to the young man that he was
well on the way to the kingdom, for Christ's reply dealt with
the observing of commandments. These, the young man said,
he had scrupulously kept. And to all outward appearances
this may have been more true than we would tend to give
him credit. But Christ cuts through the shallow outward

observance of the law. He begins with the first of all commandments,—"Thou shalt have no other gods before me."
At this point the young man's status collapses. "One thing
thou lackest," said Jesus. The young ruler *does* have other
gods before the true God. Tested directly at this point, "his
countenance fell, and he went away sorrowful; for he had
great possessions."

It must have come as a considerable shock to this "toast
of the younger set," the pride of the community," the "catch
of the year" to discover that he was farther from the kingdom than he had ever dreamed. Now in sadness he understood that the way of a man to the heart of God is through
the evident willingness to surrender all other loves to a first
love for God. His love, like that of many, lay in things material. Just "one thing" stood in the way of his reach for the
kingdom, but that "one thing" was the greatest of all.

The rich young ruler of Jesus' day has his counterparts
in our day as well. They live in your town and mine. To all
appearances nicer people cannot be found. They, too, match
up to every demand of men. "If they are not fit for the kingdom, then who is?" we ask. And Christ answers, "If any man
would come after me, let him deny himself and take up his
cross and follow me. For whosoever would save his life shall
lose it, and whosoever loses his life shall find it. For what will
it profit a man if he gains the whole world and forfeits his
life?" Just "one thing" can make all the difference.

A Wastebasket for Memories

A STAGNATING CHRISTIANITY will soon be no Christianity at all, for the Christian life is more than just *being;* it is a *becoming* and a *growing.* I recall this truth almost automatically whenever I read Paul's letter to his Philippian friends. He said: "Not that I have already obtained this (becoming like Christ) or am already perfect; but I press on to make it my own . . . Brethren, I do not consider that I have made it my own; but *one thing I do,* forgetting what lies behind and straining forward to what lies ahead, I press on toward the goal for the prize of the upward call of God in Christ Jesus."

Very few men have known better than the Apostle Paul the danger of a stagnating Christianity and the contrasting power to be found in a Christian life that presses on. It is so easy for us to become complacent with the gift of our salvation. That gift *is* a remarkable thing. It involves our spiritual birth. But it is only the beginning. Christ wants us to "grow up" as well.

For anyone satisfied alone with spiritual birth, Paul's salvation. That gift *is* a remarkable thing. It involves our spiritual birth. But it is only the beginning. Christ wants us to est missionary of all times? Was he not the writer of the New Testament letters? Looking at this we might be tempted to believe that Paul, too, thought himself to have arrived spiritually. This was not so. Paul knew that his salvation was assured through faith in Christ but that his growing process would involve the length of his days.

A great editor once said that the secret of being a successful editor lay in knowing what to throw into the wastebasket. May I suggest that there may be a parallel here in reference to growth in the Christian life? Paul suggests this. Knowing what to hang on to and what to be rid of, what to forget, is important.

When Paul penned those unusually well-remembered phrases "One thing I do . . . I press on . . . ," he inserted between the two another quite unexpected phrase which reads "forgetting what lies behind . . . " Are you surprised?

Paul had wrestled with the haunting memory of past sins. His personal record was not a pretty one. He had been the famous persecutor of Christians. He had stood by when the first Christian martyr in history was stoned without a single defender. He had dragged Christian families out of homes and into jails. No wonder that he once said, "I am not worthy to be called an apostle." But suppose that he had lived constantly with these memories and with such a conclusion. He could not have grown spiritually. He could not possibly have become the dynamic Christian personality he was, beloved by all the Christian world.

Now it is equally true that you cannot spend your time in the cemetery of your past forgiven sins, dig up the bones, look them over, and still expect to grow in your spiritual life. Christ has promised that "if we confess our sins, he is faithful and just, and will forgive our sins and cleanse us from all unrighteousness." He means that. He has given us a wastebasket for the memories of past forgiven sin.

Gift for Eternity

AN INTERESTING TRUE STORY comes out of Dallas, Texas, from the typewriter of Patricia Reel of the United Press. A Texan woman made a small fortune, then gave it away. She is a seventy-three-year-old teacher who could not realize her ambition to do missionary work but has donated a hundred thousand dollars that others might go to foreign lands.

The teacher, Mrs. Lillian Nelson, has lived all her life without most of the luxuries many of her friends take for granted. She has devoted herself to the Baptist Church. The San Antonio woman and her late husband, Joseph Edward Nelson, both taught school. It was their habit to save part of their small income. They did not buy new cars, took few vacations and wore made-over clothes. After years of skimpy living, they saved up five thousand dollars and invested it in steel company stock. The school-teaching couple built this investment into a fortune but never used it for themselves. Mrs. Nelson's small home in San Antonio is simple and functional with roll-rugs rather than wall-to-wall carpeting.

This remarkably unselfish woman was born in a small town in southwest Texas. At the age of thirteen she joined a small Baptist church at Cold Springs. Mrs. Nelson, who has been a Baptist Sunday School teacher for 55 years, first learned about missions at the family altar in her father's home. Mrs. Nelson recalls, "We had a big farm house with a fireplace, and Dad delighted in getting us all around him to listen to the Scripture." She adds, "We did not have any money then. Cotton was five cents a pound. But tithing and foreign missions were entrenched in our memory. We had some cattle and some hogs and sheep and we always knew that the Lord would get the fattest yearling or the best lamb."

In what she lightly calls her "spare-time" Mrs. Nelson putters in the garden, tries her hand at interior decorating, ceramic work and painting, raises goldfish, sews, reads and cooks. As Mrs. Nelson put it when she gave this gift, "If I can't personally go to the foreign mission field, then it is my duty to make provision for those who can go." When she signed the annuity papers, Mrs. Nelson said, "Who knows what things this gift may make possible. Maybe some day in heaven many a little boy will come up to me and say, 'You made it possible for me to be here'."

And that is a warm-hearted story for our kind of world, isn't it? It's a gift for eternity.

Be Still and Know

LET ME BEGIN by telling you of an experience that my wife and I had with our children on a vacation several summers ago. We were staying at a cottage by the side of one of the many lakes in Waupaca's Chain of Lakes in Wisconsin. Among other things that we had done was to rent a canoe. I had always enjoyed one and I found that my family did, too. My wife and I would take positions on the seats in each end of the canoe, with our daughters on the floor, and paddle our way along the lake shore.

I shall never forget the experience of one afternoon. It had been a beautiful day, silver blue skies overhead with a few fleecy clouds, a somewhat variable wind, depending upon which lake we were on and whether the shoreline was high and well protected by the trees, or lower to give the wind an opportunity to hit the surface of the lake and to stir it into waves and ripples.

As we moved from one lake into another, we found that each lake took on a different character. Half way through a narrow connecting channel, I turned the canoe sharply to the left, directly toward the trees and the shoreline, where suddenly appeared at the bow of the canoe a tiny little outlet almost hidden by the grass and the brush. Entering it we could move through another narrow channel which after some yards brought us out upon a very beautiful, serene little lake. There was not a cottage on it. Turtles were sunning themselves on logs with lily pads to right and to left. It was as we found ourselves on this quiet lake that there came to me a phrase out of one of the Psalms, the fortysixth. "Be still and know that I am God."

Everyday life is like that experience of ours on those several lakes, with the variations in wind and the roughness of water. Life holds so many different things—happiness and sadness, trouble and success, fear and confidence. But if life is going to hold most of confidence and success, strength and courage, faith and stability,—how important that you and I begin each day with "Be still and know that I am God."

When Your Heart's on Fire

I WONDER if you can remember the feeling that came over you when as a little boy or girl you stepped through the door to the Christmas tree and found under it just what you had been dreaming about for many weeks.

Or, I wonder how well some of you remember the emotion you felt when the wedding march began, when the moment for which you had so long waited was there. Only minutes, and standing side by side you heard the words which declared you to be husband and wife.

Or, do you recall, some of you, the moment when a nurse stepped through a much-watched door to say, "It's a boy," or "It's a girl?" How to picture that feeling which is ours may not always be quite so simple. But perhaps I have found a phrase which describes such emotional experiences better than almost any other. It is not my phrase. The fact of the matter is, it is God's. He put it on the lips of a couple of very ordinary men who on the evening of that first Easter Day underwent one of the most unique experiences that has ever come to any man. Here they were, two downhearted men, followers of Jesus Christ, who felt thoroughly licked because they knew nothing as yet of Easter's real glory. They had left the city gates of Jerusalem and were shuffling down the road to a little village about eight miles away, called Emmaus. They had left the city, but they had not left their memories of the past days behind. These were only too vivid.

There was that night trial when their friend and leader, Jesus, was railroaded into the hands of Pilate, the governor, for a judgment of death. There was the scene outside the city gates where their dear friend was crucified between two criminals. There was the slow walk to Joseph's tomb in the garden where His still and lifeless body was laid behind a huge stone which closed the grave. What an end Jesus had come to!

And what an end they had come to, hoping that this One had been He who should redeem their people. The Man was dead, and what's more, it was the third day. Some of this thinking they had shared out loud, for the two men had been joined by a third as they trudged along that road in the gloomy twilight. The third had wanted to know what caused their gloom, as though He should not have known if His eyes and ears had been open at all around Jerusalem that weekend. Peculiar though, He seemed to know a great deal at that. He was even a bit harsh. He said, " 'O fools and slow of heart to believe all that the prophets have spoken: Ought not Christ to have suffered these things and entered into glory?' And beginning at Moses and all the prophets, he expounded unto them in all the scriptures, the things concerning himself."

Now they had arrived at Emmaus. It was already late, too late surely for their road companion to go on. So they invited Him in, and there at supper, as He took bread, blessed it and broke it, their eyes were suddenly opened to the wonderful fact that this Man who had walked by their side, had talked with them, was none other than their leader and friend

Jesus—not dead, not a futile hope, not a dream exploded, but living, real, and risen.

Then He was suddenly gone from them. I wonder if you or I can even begin to imagine the looks on their faces. I wonder if we could have even the faintest notion of what it must have been like for them to rush out of the little cottage and hurry down the dark road back to Jersualem. "Did not our heart burn within us, while He talked with us by the way, and while He opened to us the scriptures?" Burning hearts! Hearts on fire!

Hearts really catch on fire and stay lighted permanently; yes, for eternity in fact, in only one experience of life—that of meeting, walking with and talking to Jesus Christ, our Living Lord. I should like to suggest further that those men and women from out of the past who really knew what they were here for, who really knew what life was all about, who really knew where they were going and found going there a wonderful experience, were the men and women with a burning heart for Jesus Christ.

Friends, that is the privilege of every one of us, the privilege of being men and women afire, men and women of the burning heart.

Hold Thou Thy cross before my closing eyes,

Shine through the gloom and point me to the skies;

Heaven's morning breaks, and earth's vain shadows flee;

In life, in death, O Lord, abide with me.

No one pens such words but he who has walked and talked along life's road with Jesus, the Living Christ. For He it is who sets a heart on fire, having blotted out all sin, erasing fear and self and pride—and points men's hearts to heaven.

Bring Your Own Light

PRESIDENT EISENHOWER, with the push of a button in his office in the White House, has set aglow the Christmas tree in Washington. Among the things that he underscored in his Christmas talk were the spiritual qualities so all-important in a nation; the fact that we must see by faith; that it is by the light of Christian charity and Christian peace that we enter into a new year. What lights for living are you bringing into the new year?

This brings to mind a speech that was given by a business man back in December of 1950, printed then, and reprinted in the Council Letter of the Economic Council of 1956.

Here is what Ellsworth Rowsey has to say: "Seated on a hotel court high in the Swiss Alps we were suddenly conscious of the distant ringing of a church bell. In response to an inquiry the proprietor of the hotel pointed to a beautiful little church with a tall stately steeple high upon a cliff some distance away.

"Twilight was fast fading into darkness, but still there was no light in the church. A guest asked a second question. If there were to be a service of worship, why were there no lights in the church? 'Oh', said the proprietor, 'that is a very interesting story. In a few minutes you will see people wending their way toward the church, each one carrying a light. The man who gave the church to this community, gave it with the understanding that there was never to be any artificial lighting in the church, but each attendant was to provide his own light. So the custom is for everybody to bring with him, when he comes to divine service, a lighted candle of his own.'

"It was only a few minutes until we saw the little lights flickering along on the paths high up on the side of the Alps. We could see the people wending their way toward the little house of worship. At first there was only a flickering light in the church, then it grew brighter until presently it was streaming out through the gorgeous stained glass windows. The whole building was a blaze of light. The service became a beacon of light in the community, because of the light of each member that was carried into it.

"John gives us the simplest and profoundest interpretation of the meaning of the birth of Christ. 'In Him was life and the light that was the light of men.' Here we have the revelation of the true light of Christmas. A simple declaration containing only twelve words of one syllable each. Three of the words are used twice in this brief sentence. Simple, yes, but one of the most comprehensive and profound declarations of the gospel. The key words are 'life' and 'light' both of which have their source in Him. What a sobering text for our time. It is spoken by the Master Himself, 'I am the light of the world, he that followest me shall not walk in darkness, but shall have the light of life.' He taught us how to rid the world of race hatred, economic injustice, aggressions, slavery and exploitation. He taught that we cannot be false to His principles and be at peace with ourselves or our world. He is a figure of world prominence for His principles will save the world. What a tragedy that at Christmas time He should so often be given second place only to Santa Claus!

"Christmas then reveals that Christ is not a chance item in the world's affairs but the revelation of the eternal purpose of God working itself out in human history. His teachings must be seen not as the mouthings of a deluded fanatic nor the impossible dreams of a visionary, but as the message of a teacher sent from God who has spoken the words of eternal life to the world. The heart of Christmas is Christ, not a luxury, but a necessity."

Have you a light to carry? You are a rare individual on the American scene if the opportunity has not come to you to know that "Light of Life." And knowing Him makes all the difference, for His light becomes yours, and you too will have a light to bring.

"Christianity works while infidelity talks. She feeds the hungry, clothes the naked, visits and cheers the sick, and seeks the lost, while infidelity abuses here and babbles nonsense and profanity. 'By their fruits ye shall know them!' "

Licked By Circumstance?

"GOD GAVE me eyes that I might thrill
To the rising sun beyond the hill
A stately pine, a bird in flight,
Or the magic of the starlit night.

God gave me ears to know the thrush,
The startled partridge in the brush,
To hear the patter of tiny feet
Tripping and dancing along the street.

God gave men hands to till the earth,
To weigh the gleanings, know their worth,
To feel the handclasp of a friend
In truth and loyalty to blend.

God gave me tongue that I proclaim
His lavish blessings and His name
To teach some stranger by the way
To see and hear and feel and pray."

So writes Frank St. Way, but what if the individual who reads
these words or hears them does not have the blessing of
sight, of hearing, of hands that move or a tongue that can
speak? Then what? Can such an individual still live above the

difficult circumstances of life?

Some weeks ago I received a letter from a very interesting personality. Some of what she writes I would like to pass on to you. She said.

"I had best explain a bit about myself. I have been confined to a wheelchair for a number of years because of arthritis. I have been almost completely disabled. I have had arthritis since I was six years old and will be celebrating my thirty-first birthday in May of this year. Yes, it is rather a long time for a young person to be physically handicapped but, with time and learning, I have found I can enjoy life just as fully as anyone else. Sometimes I am even aware of feeling that I have an edge over some normal healthy people when it comes to living and enjoying life to the greatest degree possible. During the cold winter months, such as now, I am very much a stay-at-home type of person; but when warm days arrive, I am able to get out and go places with the able assistance of relatives or friends. Letter-writing, reading, music and TV are some of the past-times I enjoy. In spite of many limitations in my life, most days pass by quickly and pleasantly. I have learned the meaning of walking with the Lord each and every day."

That is an inspiring letter, is it not? For we are reminded out of it that you may choose to be whipped by circumstances or be triumphant over them, depending on whether you choose to believe in destiny by circumstances or in the promises of God. The promises of God are many, if you and I will hear them. "My grace is sufficient for you." "I can do all things through Christ who strengthens me." "Be strong in the Lord and in the power of His might." Are you licked by circumstances or victorious through the promises of God?

Life's Common Denominator

OUR RADIO ANNOUNCER had a chuckle for us in the news through the story of the "minnow-matic" invented by a gentleman in Mitchell, South Dakota. It is an apparatus that dispenses on a conveyor minnows for the fisherman with the deposit of a quarter. Then he added an additional chuckle when he suggested that perhaps the next real need is for an automatic dispensing machine that would make it possible to have delivered into your hand, with the dropping of a quarter, a minnow that is already put on a hook; that perhaps the ladies particularly would enjoy this. I suppose about the only thing you could add to that again would be a system where a fisherman dozing in a boat could have a fish tossed automatically up into the boat for him. We are only kidding, of course; and we take our hats off to somebody with a new idea.

But perhaps this lazy-way invention may suggest to us something a bit more serious. It is the tendency in our day to become more lazy than perhaps we really ought to be, to water down the level of our talents and our abilities to the lowest common denominator rather than to use the two, five or ten-talent abilities that the Almighty God has given to us.

This is the story of two friends as told by Paul W. Brauer of Boston. Simon and Arturio lived in a little village in Italy,

not far from Palermo. They were humble but contented goat
shepherds. One day Simon heard about a wonderful new
idea which the wise men of the world were trying to intro-
duce. These wise men had concluded that God wanted all
men to live on the same level and that all good people ought
to do something about it. Simon was very much impressed
by it all. This was a project for him and for his good friend
Arturio, whom he immediately won over.

Sitting on the hillside, the two friends surveyed the orange
groves in the valley below. Pointing with his finger, Simon
called the attention of Arturio to a particularly well-kept
orange grove. "You see," he said, "that is the grove of
Gabriel. He has thirty orange trees while his neighbors have
only a dozen. Let's do something about it."

Arturio enthusiastically agreed to cooperate with his
friend, though apparently they did not understand each
other. On the next day Simon lustily swung his axe in the
grove of Gabriel until all but a dozen trees had been chopped
down. Then he went in search for his turn-coat friend Arturio. He found him in a neighbor's garden. "Arturio," he
said, "I thought we had agreed to create equality among
these villagers."

"But that's just what I am doing, Simon." replied Arturio.
"See, I have planted eighteen new trees in the garden of
these poor people."

It is one thing to level everybody down to the lowest
common denominator and quite another to take our talents
and abilities and with loving concern try to help not only
ourselves but others to live on the level of ability and opportunity that the Almighty God has given. In this, serving God
and serving fellow man, we find our satisfactions.

Citizen of Two Worlds

A POPULAR SONG introduced in 1956 included these interesting words: "we live in two worlds, we will make the two worlds one." However romantic or unromantic you may feel, the quoted phrases do have sound scriptural backing. You may remember the words of our Lord, "Have you not read that he who made them from the beginning made them male and female, and said 'For this reason shall a man leave his father and mother and be joined to his wife, and the two shall become one?' "

Anyone who has discovered the wonder of love and marriage "going together like a horse and carriage" has found that it puts two people from two "worlds" of their own into one they share in common.

But these are not the only worlds that people are trying to bring together. Wendell Wilkie, some years ago, used as a theme the phrase "One World". What he was trying to register on our consciousness was that this physical world of ours, 25,000 miles around, was shrinking by the day; that we did not live far apart geographically any more. Further, he wanted us to be aware that each nation living in its own self-interested little world must become a part of one unified, cohesive world with men and nations not at odds but at peace with each other; common needs pressing us to common goals resulting in common hopes. But how?

There is yet another area where men and nations live in two worlds which need urgently to be reconciled, two worlds extremely far apart which God would have to be one world, one kingdom. Scripture speaks of them often,—the world around us composed of things material, physical, educational, cultural and political, and then that great eternal world of the spirit, the Kingdom of God. Here of necessity citizens of the one, of nation and country, we as Christians are also citizens of the other—God's kingdom. How difficult it is, even for the Christian, to reconcile these two citizenships, for they are so often at odds.

Peter, James and John had this problem when they were thrown into prison for preaching the Gospel in the face of forbidding orders from the local authorities. The disciples' resolution of the matter is known by their statement, "We must obey God rather than men." Their prior allegiance lay in the Kingdom eternal.

The Apostle Paul speaks often of the "two worlds." In reference to his citizenship in the Roman Empire, he indicates a pardonable pride. He also used that citizenship to advantage in his appeal to Caesar. And it was respected.

At the same time, however, citizen of Rome that he was, his citizenship in the kingdom of heaven was determinative of his life and conduct. To Paul, his citizenship in heaven, his allegiance to Christ, was a base, a foundation, which if fully shared by his fellow men would make possible the establishment of the highest order of human society. To Paul, the great tensions in human affairs—man with man, and nation with nation—grew out of man's enmity with and estrangement from God who alone can make of all nations one people.

Paul, then, sought out the best in the physical world and

human society of which he was a citizen but determined the
course of his conduct, the plan of his life, according to the
King of Kings, Jesus Christ. He wrote:—"Be not conformed
to this world but be transformed by the renewal of your mind,
that you may prove what is the will of God, what is good and
acceptable and perfect."

Brooded By Love

SCARCELY A DAY goes by but what in newspapers or over the air we catch some indication of the problems that are being faced by the young people of our community. Moste often when we speak of these they fall under the terminology of juvenile delinquency. A report that came out of the Senate sub-committee making a study of juvenile delinquency in America, includes the following paragraph:

"The emotional atmosphere, the hostilities and the inadequacies expressed in the parent-child relationships do greater injury to the child than do his physical hurts. From a preventive point of view then, it seems clear that the greatest hope for discouraging delinquency lies in efforts to improve the quality and harmony of the family system."

When adults come to such a conclusion, you might find it very interesting to see what the conclusions are on the part of a group of young people out of Seattle, Washington, public schools, who have ideas of their own. They prepared a statement that was called "When parents fill these basic needs, delinquency hasn't a chance." Their statement holds suggestions not only for parents but for many types of workers in the children's field who need to gain the respect and confidence of youngsters. Here were their suggestions.

First of all, they named love. "Home is where people love

each other. We want to be sure our parents will love us no matter what happens."

Secondly, they named understanding. "We want parents we can take troubles to and be sure they'll understand. Some parents won't listen or let their children explain."

Then, trust. "Our parents could trust us more than they often do. They should tell us what we need to know about dating without being old-fashioned."

Then, joint-planning. "We want parents who realize we are growing up and who stand beside us, not over us—the kind who are ready to talk things over instead of just trying to boss us."

And, respect. "We want our parents to respect us and treat us like teen-age people, not little children."

And, privacy. "We want parents who are interested in what we are doing but not nosey, who don't listen in on the phone or look through our letters or personal effects."

And, responsibility. "We want to do our share of family tasks and duties, but why can't we talk over who is to do what and why?"

And, then, religion. "It's good to feel our parents have a religion they are sincerely trying to live right in the family and everywhere else. It's really nice to have grace at meals and for the whole family to go to church. It makes us feel we really belong and gives us something to build on."

Having read that once, you may find yourself reading it again, very appreciative of some highly mature thinking. I concluded that these young people had pin-pointed the issues of critical importance and had asked for that to which a teen-ager might well be entitled.

In a far earlier period in American history, when life for youth may (or, perhaps to our surprise, may not) have been quite different, Henry Ward Beecher penned it well when he wrote: "If God has taught us all truth in teaching us to love, then he has given us an interpretation of our whole duty to our households. We are not born as the partridge in the wood, or the ostrich of the desert, to be scattered everywhere; but we are to be grouped together, and brooded by love, and reared day by day in that first of churches,— the family."

Diluted Qualities

EVERY SO OFTEN both in national and international circles we do some talking about the disarmament of our war power. I suspect that there are few of us who do not give some very deep concern to this. At the same time we doubt that we have any perfect or pat answer for it, particularly inasmuch as this problem deals with nations which are so varied in their thinking, in their ideals and in their religious beliefs or lack of them.

Samuel T. Williamson once said, "War is a dirty business. It plumbs the depths of degradation yet demands the best that one can give. In the last war what I did and what I saw did not rest easily on my memory; but in all the filth and stupidities of that experience I saw courage, fortitude, sacrifice, self-abnegation, generosity, yes, and tenderness, compassion and idealism of a quality that I have not seen since. It is because these qualities become diluted in peacetime that wars return."

The return of wars upon each succeeding generation is like a man who began to lose his hair. It grew thinner and thinner until finally he had but one hair left. He brushed that hair, combed and shampooed it, and faithfully nurtured it. One morning he awoke, looked down upon his pillow and there was the hair. He exclaimed, "What now? I'm bald!"

It is that way with war. It comes upon us gradually over many years. We may wake up and find ourselves thrust suddenly into it, but the roots of that war lie way back in the motives and habits and institutions of mankind.

Does this not suggest to us that perhaps one of the great difficulties that we so often have as we wrestle with the problem of international relationships and war is that we do not work nearly as hard at peace in peacetime as we work at war in wartime?

What are some of the costs of war? We are informed that for all the nations combined, World War II cost a trillion dollars—that is a thousand billion dollars. We are further informed that for this sum every family in the world could have had a new six-room house and a car, and every town of five thousand a new hospital and a new high school.

We ask, "Who is to blame?" and often unconsciously begin with the most ridiculous of all—God. An Englishman once said to another as they took shelter in a raid, "Why doesn't God stop this awful war?" Replied the second, "He didn't start it."

We ought to remind ourselves that God is not an earthly king sitting on a human throne issuing mandates to one and then another,—taking sides by whim or fancy. He does issue a law of love, in which law men must live in accord—or die. While God's laws of love or judgment slowly work their way, men will suffer for blundering willfulness, mistaken judgments and wrong actions. But should man learn to live in harmony with divine law, which means in harmony with God and love, then wars would cease.

God is love. It is not physical might and power that will solve the problems of the world. Holy Scripture has yet to be refuted. "Not by might nor by power, but by my Spirit," says the Lord. In this lies the answer to the struggles of men.

What then confronts the concerned man? It is this. If we as nations involuntarily took the loss of a trillion dollars in armament, destruction, and sheer waste as the dollar price of World War II; if we gave up the cream of our youth to wasted years, to dislocation, to injury, brutality and death— if we saw courage, sacrifice, generosity, tenderness, compassion placed so generously on the altars of war; then ought we not ask what measure of these we are willing to invest during our moments of peace in order to retain that peace?

Dollars are involved, but to a lesser degree than we suspect. For while dollars may be visible tokens of love when given, yet they cannot purchase with assurance either absolute material security or moral conscience or human understanding. Should you remove God and His will from the scene, then there is left no alternative but dollars for military might coupled with shrewdest diplomacy. But this we have tried. And in this we have failed. Here lies no peace.

Where then lies the answer? It lies in this;—the channeling of these undiluted Christian attributes of love, of courage, of sacrifice; of generosity and tenderness and compassion into international relationship in the name of "Christ who is our peace." All other methods have failed. History records the failures in detail. Only if the nations of the earth know Christ and live His law of love will there be peace. If this is not our hope, there is none other. If this be true, a diluted Christianity will not do.

Successful Failures

THE CITY OF Minneapolis with other American communities annually observes Crime Prevention Week. Quite regularly it falls in observance time with Boy Scout Sunday and by coincidence with National Brotherhood week as well. Each of these evidence some specific concerns on our part for human relationships in our community and nation. But we do not always follow through in, of all places, our homes.

Last fall I went to the State Fair with my youngsters. I was literally compelled by one of them who has a particular love for animals to visit the barns, but most particularly to see the horses. My compelling youngster has always loved animals, and horses top the list. She would have a horse stabled in our garage if the choice were hers.

We did see some very handsome horses,—skillfully groomed, curried and cared for by those who love those horses and were seeking prizes at the Fair. We also looked in on some very beautifully groomed pigs. There was one with a prize blue ribbon. It had been cared for as though it were a lady in a beauty shop—one of the most beautiful looking pigs (if you can imagine it) that you might ever hope to see. But, as I stood looking into the stall where this pig was, I noted a rather peculiar contrast. A little boy was also there. He was a very thin, unkempt, emaciated looking youngester, his hair grown much too long. I discovered that the youngster, as scrawny and unhealthy as he looked, had the same master as the pig.

We live in a world where we are tempted altogether too often to become confused in our values. We live in the busy world of competition where success is more important than anything else. The problem that we face is that of trying to meet the competitive world; to stay in business; "to stay on top," as we say; and yet in this setting to give the kind of care we ought to our own children.

The whole future rests on our youngsters. We know this but we are not the first ones to become confused. King David was one of the most successful kings of all history. He was a great statesman. A great leader of the army and a man beloved by his people, he had welded a group of rather varied people together in loyalty and esteem. But he was a failure as a father. There came a day when his son died. Then he had this to conclude, "My son, my son, would God that I had died for thee."

Are we successful failures as parents? Sometimes we are. Perhaps this is one of the issues involved in the whole business of crime prevention and building a better tomorrow.

Larger, Larger, Larger!

Each Easter Sunday millions of Americans find their way through church doors throughout our land. From out of their worship experience they come away with another re-emphasis upon the great truth that has transformed human kind over a great many years.

Winston Churchill, writing about Lawrence of Arabia, once used a word picture which, transferred, I think might fit exceedingly well the atmosphere that the Christian ought to discharge in the world of our day when he knows and assumes for himself the great truth of Easter. Churchill says that part of the secret of Lawrence of Arabia's power lay in his disdain for most of the pleasures and comforts of life. He said, "The world actually looks with some awe on a man who appears unconcerned and indifferent to money, comfort, rank, power and fame. The world feels without certain apprehension that here is someone who is outside its jurisdiction, someone before whom allurements may be spread in vain, someone strangely untamed and untrammeled by convention and moving independently of the ordinary currents of human action."

A man can do that if he has an understanding of life that has carried him over and beyond the secular and the material aspects of it. We cannot live with very much freedom in our souls if we are tied only to things material and to nothing beyond. Robert Louis Stevenson once said, "God, if this were faith—to go on forever and fail and to go on again and to be mauled to the earth and arise and contend for the shade of a word and a thing not seen with the eyes, Lord, if that were enough . . . "

A great sea captain of many years ago had a different kind of thought as over against one of his men whose life was lost when he was serving aboard ship. Around the Cape Horn a seaman was killed on deck. It was the Swedish custom to address the dead in a final service as if he were living. And the captain of the vessel addressed the lad in this way: "Ronald Walker, here we are gathering all your old ship-mates together to bid you a last farewell. And this is a better day for you than it is for us. This earth in which we still re-main, from which you have been called, this earth of ours is just a testing place and, when we have proved ourselves, we shall come. Here we are just children going through our schooling. You have qualified. You lived worthily. You sleep well, nor will you awaken upon the Cape Horn road. You will awaken in glory with eternity before you. The voice that calls upon the last day will reach you here lying in your cold and unmarked grave as clearly as it will those who sleep on land."

It makes a difference whether we have caught the mean-ing of the eternal. Michelangelo, the great artist, stood with a critical eye before a canvas that had been done by Raphael. Raphael was still a student then, and as Michaelangelo ex-amined it, he took a chalk and scrawled across the whole canvas the words "amplius, amplius, amplius"—"larger, larger, larger!" Life needs to be larger, beyond the here and now and the things we can touch. It must reach to God and out into eternity.

How pathetic if it is lived otherwise so that one comes to the end of life and complains bitterly, as Talleyrand did when he said, "Behold eighty-three years passed away; What cares! What agitation! What anxieties! What ill-will! What sad complications! And all without any other result except great fatigue of body and mind, and disgust with regard to the past, and a profound sentiment of discouragement and despair with regard to the future."

How about you? Has the fact of Easter pushed out the horizon of your life so that you find it possible to live outside the jurisdiction of the world and its conventions? Have you found life an abundant venture into God's kingdom as a result?

"Now to him who by the power at work within us is able to do far more abundantly than all that we ask or think, to him be glory . . . "

For Which There Is
No Substitute

A SENATE SUB-COMMITTEE has warned us that by 1965 a million teen-age lawbreakers will come before the courts unless the entire nation joins in the effort to curb mounting juvenile delinquency. The Senate "Juvenile Delinquency Sub-committee" said that the answer to the problem lies in better schools, more recreational facilities and a sharp drive to wipe out the narcotics traffic. Senator Hennings, a Democrat of Missouri who succeeded Senator Kefauver, added, "Of course, as everyone realizes, juvenile delinquency is a problem which must be solved almost entirely by state and local authorities."

This is all well and good. You and I have a great amount of respect for those in positions of authority in our land who are concerned about juvenile delinquency. But I am wondering if perhaps there are not some other answers that we may tend to overlook.

Many of you read the comics and I do, too,—at least part of the time. I noted this in the comic-strip "Juliet Jones." Julie is putting to bed a girl she has befriended, not a youngster but a young adult who has become very mixed up. She says, "There, snug as a bug in a rug. Need anything else?" "Need anything else!" says the girl. "Oh, Julie, if only somebody had asked me if I needed anything else when I was a little girl. If just one human being had shown me just a thou-

sandth of the kindness you are showing me now, then maybe
I wouldn't be so strangled with the craziest kind of feelings
that make me want to shut out everything and everybody in this
whole mixed up, cruel world!"

Perhaps by contrast that takes us to another headline.
A former U. S. Senator today was named the "1957 American
Mother of the Year." She is Mrs. Hazel Able of Lincoln,
Nebraska, who exclaimed, "It is the greatest honor I have
ever had, even greater than serving in the Senate." This takes
us right back home, does it not? It suggests that our greatest
strengths and our most critically important areas of life lie
in our homes with Dads and Moms and this treasure called
love. For it is love which ever gives, forgives, outlives and
ever stands with open hands. While love lives it freely gives,
for this is love's prerogative. And no recipient will ever be
the same as one to whom love has been a stranger.

"Love is patient and kind; love is not jealous or boast-
ful; it is not arrogant or rude. Love does not insist on its own
way; it is not irritable or resentful; it does not rejoice at
wrong, but rejoices in the right. Love bears all things, believes all things, hopes all things, endures all things."

Angels in the Outfield

SOME YEARS AGO a movie was made of the book *Angels in the Outfield*. The closing scene of the picture shows a baseball diamond in the twilight hours after the baseball game is over. The crowds have left the stand. The players have retired to their dressing rooms and by now they too have left the stadium. There is no one in the park visible to the eye, but voices are heard coming from out of the past,— voices of some of the great immortals of baseball fame who are calling, "Let's play ball." The "baseball chatter" of the short stop calling to the outfielder and the catcher talking to the batter comes through the eerie quietness.

It is an imaginary scene. Yet in a sense it suggests the unseen world that surrounds us and steps out of the past into the present. You and I are brought to a realization of the fact that we do not live our lives in an isolated manner. What you and I say and think and do is reflected in the lives of others and what others have said and thought and done before us is likewise reflected in our lives today.

What is your or my relationship to our fellow man? Do we find selfless devotion and love in the picture of our work today? Though you or I perhaps make the poorest appraisals of all in measuring our own worth, erring in the direction of too much modesty or too little humility, the question is worth the asking and asking most honestly. What of my family, what of my church, what of my associates, what of the world about me,—because I live, because I am around? Have these gained while I have lived or have they been robbed of a better happiness that they might have had with someone else around? Have these known an easier life or a harder life? Have these walked a smoother road or a rougher road? Have these known more smiles or fewer? Have these known more courage or less strength? Have these grown or become more dwarfed because of me?

Ours is a very needy world. It is in need of love-filled men and women as perhaps it has never before needed them. It needs just plain "quality folk," whose greatest asset is the spirit of Jesus Christ. Say what we will, it is a fact that you and I belong either to the makers or the breakers of our homes, our churches, our communities and of the world. Some of us may be frozen assets, not too much of anything. Some of us may be humble love-carriers for Christ to the men around us, however simple our style. Some of us perhaps would not add up to too much in the "plus" department in this world of men. It is important that we do, for this world needs the spirit of Jesus Christ lived out in men touching the lives of others day in, day out, seven days a week.

An Unconscious Loss of Power

A SKILLED TEACHER with the rare ability to illustrate truths in simple but colorful ways is an inspiration to any class or audience. Jesus Christ was such a Master Teacher. He had to an incomparable degree the unique ability to light up His pupil's understanding by using the common things of every day as parallels, contrasts or visual pictures of His spoken words. There was the farmer planting his seed. There were the birds that flew over head. He used as illustrations the trees, the vines and the manner in which they grew. He drove home a lesson with His reference to a house built on a sand pile. He used the very ordinary in an extraordinary way to make the profound more easily understood.

This which we have seen in Jesus as a teacher has also helped us to learn by imaginative observation. One of my lessons was learned one day in a Springfield, Missouri, garage. I had driven in to have something of a minor nature taken care of. The mechanic made the adjustment, then raced the motor to check on the results. As he listened, he suggested a more careful examination of the motor. He tested the compression on each of the cylinders and found that two of them were down to a feeble twenty pounds. The valves were too far gone for grinding and had to be replaced.

When the car had been repaired and I drove out of the garage and down the street, I was surprised at the surging power under the hood. The "pick-up" was startling. Yet this car's speed and power were not wholly new to me. I had experienced them before when the car was new. But, because of a very gradual loss in efficiency, I had forgotten what once had been. It was an unconscious loss of power.

There is a way in which many of God's people have experienced something very similar. One of the Old Testament Judges illustrates this particularly well. You recall the story. His name was Samson.

A whole nation had been astonished at his feats of strength. He had torn off the city gates of Gaza in scorn only to plant them at the top of a high hill. For the children of Israel, Samson was a one-man army and a judge for more than twenty years. Enemies trembled at the thought of him. They ran at the sight of him. His name, then and since, has stood synonymous with strength.

But Samson is representative of something else as well. Whether it was pride before a fall or the belief that in his highly regarded position he was exempt from obedience to God,—Samson played with fire, lived lustfully as the soon unwitting pawn of Delilah. Trapped in spiritual weakness, he also lost his physical prowess. " . . . I will go out as at other times, and shake myself free," he said. " . . . he did not know that the Lord had left him. And the Philistines seized him and gouged out his eyes . . . " Samson, the giant of giants, had experienced "an unconscious loss of power."

Many Christian men have lived with some of the same thrills in spiritual strength as were the thrills of Samson over physical might. There is a great adventure under God. But once spiritually strong men have also known humiliating, dramatic and unexpected defeats. How can one explain this?

Perhaps to the mind of man it may be explained as in

the example of my car. There was no sudden collapse which was easily detectable. There was rather an unconscious loss of power which in a moment of great stress suddenly made itself known.

Few men or women fall suddenly from spiritual heights to depths without the preliminary inner corrosion of self-sufficient pride or malnourishment of soul. "Famous" sinners attest to the truth of this: a David, a Samson, a Peter, a Judas and a host of others more contemporary than they. An unconscious loss of power is a risk none can afford.

"Watch and pray that you may not enter into temptation; the Spirit indeed is willing, but the flesh is weak." These are the words of Christ who did "watch" and did "pray" even in an hour when his self-sufficient followers slept their way into the betrayal of a life-time.

Talking to Yourself

I LEFT THE CHURCH one night and was walking down the street toward the parking lot when I heard a voice. At first I could not determine its source. Then I discovered that it was coming from a man who was approaching me from down the street. He was a tall, handsome, well-dressed man who was talking to himself. I could not hear what he was saying over the distance that separated us. Whether he was affirming some kind of a belief, whether he was rehearsing a speech, I do not know.

A good number of us talk to ourselves, at least on occasion. What we say may not be audible. What is it that we say? It is important that we ask this question, for according to what we say to ourselves, so we are. What we proclaim, consciously or unconsciously, we are.

The pessimistic philosopher is a man who finds himself always thinking and speaking in negatives. John Ruskin once said that "the quality of our inward thoughts gets itself exteriorized on our faces." Some thoughts are beautiful and some are glum. It makes a difference what it is that you and I are affirming day by day. We are either affirming life or death, joy or unhappiness, health or illness, victory, temptation, sin or defeat—any one of these things.

Pat once said to Mike, "Mike, I believe anything you tell me providing you tell me often enough." Too often you and I are telling ourselves things that are negative. The Apostle Paul, writing to a group that had been giving him some support, reminded them, "Remember that I am not utterly dependent on that offering. I would have an inner contentment regardless of outer circumstances." Napoleon, when asked about circumstances, once said, "Circumstances, bah! I make circumstances." There is a parallel here in the spirit of optimism. It was, however, in a different spirit that Paul added, "I can do all things through Christ who strengthens me." Or as often translated, "In Him who gives me the strength I am able to do anything."

What you and I are saying to ourselves makes an immeasurable difference. Whether it be vocally so others can hear it or spoken within a man's own soul, what we know and say to ourselves affirms our faith or lack of it. And this makes all the difference.

"Who shall separate us from the love of Christ? Shall tribulation, or distress, or persecution, or famine, or nakedness, or peril, or sword? As it is written, 'For thy sake we are being killed all the day long; we are regarded as sheep to be slaughtered.' So in all these things we are more than conquerors through him who loved us. For I am sure that neither death, nor life, nor angels, nor principalities, nor things present, nor things to come, nor powers, nor height, nor depth, nor anything else in all creation, will be able to separate us from the love of God in Christ Jesus our Lord."

The Road We Travel

A CHISH, KING OF GATH, once asked a rather unusual question of King David: "Whither have ye made a road today?" Many of us love old country roads. Some of the most pleasant experiences in my life have been those on a quiet country road. On occasion my wife and I have wandered away from a cabin and out on a lonely road where we could hear the distant tinkle of a cowbell and all was velvet quiet. But these moods die too and we long for broad highways on which to make our way back to the great cities.

Life is a series of roads. Robert Frost once wrote, "I shall be telling this with a sigh somewhere ages and ages hence. Two roads diverged in a wood and I—I took the one less traveled by and that has made all the difference."

It does make a difference where we walk, the roads of life that we travel. Some of them are dusty, dirty roads and some are paved, some of them easy and some of them hard. And it makes a vast amount of difference which road we take, the right road or the wrong, the smooth and easy or the rough and hard. The choices that we make reflect our character. They tell the story of what we are and who we are. "Whither have ye made a road today?"

When we move down the roads of life, we ought to leave our contributing footprint upon the world in which we live.

Dr. Paul Empie, a fine, able leader in the Lutheran Church, once wrote: "I remember reading in my Latin book when I was a kid in school a story about a Roman general. This Roman general was going into a battle that seemed almost certain defeat and his companion, who was a coward, refused to go along. So the Roman general went alone at the head of his army and, after a long bloody struggle, won a victory. He came back to his tent and threw back the flap. There sat his cowardly comrade sulking in his seat. The victor looked at him in scorn and exclaimed, 'Go kill yourself, Marcellus, we won a glorious victory and you were not there!' "

You and I are moving down the roads of life. They ought to be roads to which we add meaning. On them, under God and in the power of Jesus Christ, we should have courage to face the problems, patience to bear the heartaches, faith to face the struggles and strength to win the victories. We must be on the road which faces the foe in the thick of the struggle for God's kind of a world. "Whither have ye made a road today?"

"By faith Abraham obeyed when he was called to go out to a place which he was to receive as an inheritance; and he went out, not knowing where he was to go. By faith he sojourned in the land of promise, as in a foreign land, living in tents with Isaac and Jacob, heirs with him of the same promise. For he looked forward to the city which has foundations, whose builder and maker is God . . . These all died in faith, not having received what was promised, but having seen it and greeted it from afar, and having acknowledged that they were strangers and exiles on the earth . . . And what more shall I say? For time would fail me to tell of Gideon, Barak, Samson, Jephthah, of David and Samuel and the prophets— who through faith conquered kingdoms, enforced justice,

received promises, stopped the mouths of lions, quenched
raging fire, escaped the edge of the sword, won strength out
of weakness, became mighty in war, put foreign armies to
flight."

"Thanksliving"

I HOPE THAT YOU had a good Thanksgiving Day, together with millions of Americans, saying, "Thank you, God, for so very much" and meaning it.

It is peculiar how difficult it is to be as thankful as we ought to be. A newly arrived Hungarian refugee pictured this when he discussed the "new world" in which he found himself in our United States. He said, "I will forget after I have lived here awhile. I know I will forget." We find it easy to forget the good things that are ours at the hand of God.

Perhaps this homey story may illustrate it. Two men in a grateful mood were talking about what their early years had meant to them. They reminisced about their school days and their former teachers. One of them said, "You know, Al, Miss Dix was the finest teacher I ever had. I can't tell you what she meant to me."

Said Al, "Well, have you ever thought to tell her so?" And Bill replied, "No, it never occurred to me. I will, though," and promptly he sat down to write to her.

Not too long afterwards he received a reply from Miss Dix. It began "Dear Willie." He chuckled a bit at that for he was now balding and had somewhat of a middle-age spread. Then she continued, "I can't tell you how much your letter meant to me. I have now been retired for some time. I live in one room and, though it is nice, I sometimes find myself just a little lonely. Here I often think about the men and women who were once boys and girls in my classroom. But yours was the first letter of thanks that I have ever received. I can't tell you how much it warmed my heart. It has given me something to fill many lonely hours."

God is not a lonely soul who needs your thanks or mine in order to continue with this world of ours. But He is deserving of our gratitude. And we need to say "thank you." We need to do this in order that we might retain a right perspective, a sense of values in this world in which we live.

The Psalmist felt that way when long ago he said, "Bless the Lord, O my soul; and all that is within me, bless his holy name! Bless the Lord, O my soul, and forget not all his benefits."

Thanksgiving Day is "Thank You" day. But ought this not be the experience of exery day? We who are Americans and live in this wonderful area of the world have received more in terms of physical benefits than perhaps any others on the face of the earth. The best way in which we can say, "Thank you, God," is to live that way in our relationship to Him and to our fellow man, to live graciously and winsomely in our everyday experience so that this world will be a better world because we live in it.

The "Insignificant"

NINETEEN HUNDRED YEARS ago one of the historians in the early Christian era described a group of people like this: "an insignificant little group of folk, singing hymns on a side street." The "insignificant little group" to which he referred were, of course, the followers of Jesus. What he said was true. How insignificant they appeared to be! Some of them were hidden in meeting rooms along a side street, some of them down in catacombs under the earth. Some had been rooted out and used as prey for snarling lions in an arena while thousands, including the Emperor, watched gleefully. Others were soaked with tar and pitch and fastened to poles, then set afire to light up the garden parties of the sadistic Emperor. How insignificant this little group of Christians seemed, these followers of Jesus, and yet, what is the story today?

On Good Friday millions upon millions of people will pass through hundreds of thousands of church doors on the North American continent and in many lands beyond. On Easter morning millions more will pass through those same doors to worship Christ. Why? Because that Jesus Christ who hung on the cross and then was placed in a tomb arose from the tomb, a living Lord. All of history has changed because

of it. It is scarcely possible for us in a few words to even
begin to measure what has transpired.

Frederick K. Wentz has written a splendid book entitled
The Times Test The Church. In it he pictures what has taken
place over the years since the dawn of Christianity. He points
up the fact that there have been four periods when Christianity has held a particularly strong influence upon the world.
The first was about the year 500 A.D. This, he says, was the
first rolling wave of Christian influence. The second came
about the year 1350, the third about 1750. Then he goes on
to claim that we today, in our age, live in the time of a
fourth wave of Christian influence in the world. Dr. Wentz
suggests, however, that it is very difficult for us to know now
whether we are on the upsweep of that wave or already at the
point of its crest. Only future history can adequately measure
this. Finally he adds that although we are presently exper-
iencing this surging influence of Christianity in the world, at
the same time the Christian Church is being buffeted and
blasted by the icy winds of enmities and anti-Christian forces
on a scale never before known to the church.

What Dr. Wentz has said makes it evident that the
Christian Church today cannot take itself for granted. When
we say that, we are actually saying that *we* who are individual
members of the Church cannot take our personal faith nor
its influence in our day for granted. It means that we must
be carried back again to what took place on a hill called Calvary where a sinful world was redeemed. The Christ who
hung there said, "When I be lifted up, I will draw all men
unto me." He has that power. He has drawn men. He will
continue to draw men so long as his "insignificant little
group of folks on a side street" are significantly faithful in
telling and retelling the message of the Gospel.

In the eyes of the world, using the measuring sticks most common in a secular and materialistic age, God's people may seem insignificant. This does not really matter. The seeds of inner "revolution" are being sown for the building of His Kingdom. The gates of hell shall not prevail against it.

"The kingdom of heaven is like a grain of mustard seed which a man took and sowed in his field; it is the smallest of all seeds, but when it has grown it is the greatest of shrubs and becomes a tree, so that the birds of the air come and make nests in its branches."

A Bed Too Short

MOST OF US AT one time or another have had the disgusting experience of having our car break down on a busy street. I had pulled up to a stop sign one day when my car's engine died and would not come to life again. I crossed the street to a filling station where I arranged for a tow truck to be sent out. When I returned to the car, I found that another driver, seeing that I was in trouble, had stopped to offer me a push. I said, "Thank you very much, but I have help coming." I had no more than turned around after he had driven away when another man came along and offered his assistance, then another and another.

On the same evening I was returning home by cab when the cab's bumper locked with the bunper of the car ahead. We got out of the cab and began to do what we could. Several other drivers stopped alongside of us to ask "Can we help? Is there something we can do?" One man came with a jack in hand.

It is a wonderful thing to live in the kind of a community where people are concerned about the problems of others. This is not always true, certainly not in every area of the world. But we who live in this community can be happy about the friendly and warm spirit that we find in the hearts of many people who have discovered that life is bigger than "little me". They know that a life which is full, rich and has meaning involves itself generously in other people's lives.

There is in the Old Testament a rather interesting phrase found in the book of Isaiah. At first it may seem puzzling. It reads: "For the bed is too short to stretch oneself on it, and the covering too narrow to wrap oneself in it." These words remind us of the story of the notorious robber called Procrustes ("The Stretcher"). In his castle he had an iron bed to which he tied prisoners, fitting their limbs to the length of the bed. If prisoners were too long for the bed, he would cut off their feet and if too short, he would stretch them painfully upon it.

Life can be like a bed that is too short if it does not take in other people, their problems and their needs. For life is more than just filling our own pockets and putting clothes on our own backs and a roof over our own heads. A full life has to do with people. We find our real happiness only as we are able to bring happiness to someone else. Then our happiness comes to us reflected from the happiness brought into the life of another.

"A bed too short." Life is a bed much too short if it leaves others out. But it is also too narrow, for individual or nation, if it leaves *God* out. Sir Joseph Stamp, the British economist, speaking on world industry, commerce and finance once said, "I suspect any solution that does not stand an ethical test."

Henry W. Grady, famous editor of the Atlanta Constitution, was speaking at a dinner in Boston. He told of an experience in and near Washington, D. C. One day he looked at the great Capitol, the marble towers as the sun came through the mist, and thought that he had never seen anything finer. A day later he was a guest in a little farm home. As he sat at the table with his host's family, they bowed their heads to say, "Thank you, God, for this that we have . . . " Here was something finer, stronger than he had seen the day before. In this love of God lay the strength and the hope and the promise for tomorrow.

"Unless the Lord builds the house, those who build it labor in vain. Unless the Lord watches over the city, the watchman stays awake in vain." The bed of life is too short if it leaves others out, too narrow if it leaves God out.

Dream True

ON THE OCCASION of the last Presidential inauguration Mamie Eisenhower blinked back the tears when her husband took office for another four years. Small wonder that she blinked back tears. I can imagine that a great number of things went through her mind, not least if we remember a statement made by former President Truman when asked if he missed the White House. "I was glad to get out," he said. "The responsibility is terrific, not only for the President but for his family."

As I read this news item, I was reminded of the story of General Grant. When he was a cadet at West Point, he hated the army. There was a bill pending in Congress to disband the school. He read about it eagerly, hoping that it would be true. But one day he saw Winfield Scott, Lieutenant General of the Army and the hero of two wars, ride by in review; and he thought to himself—how wonderful it would be to ride in Scott's place. With that, a homesick cadet, tired of his military studies and drills, dreamed his dream of future honor which came true.

I do not know what dreams President Eisenhower had years ago as far as public life was concerned. But on Inauguration Day he stood before the nation and said, "I do solemnly swear that I will faithfully execute the office of the

President of the United States and will to the best of my ability preserve, protect and defend the Constitution of the United States." Then the President added, *"So help me God."*

A number of religious implications were involved in the inauguration. Perhaps you noted that the verse out of the Thirty-third Psalm upon which President Eisenhower's finger rested when he took the oath was "Blessed is the nation whose God is the Lord, the people whom he has chosen as his inheritance." It is of tremendous import to our American people that we have leaders of our nation who recognize that the task which is theirs is one so great in responsibilty that it requires the guidance and direction of the Almighty God.

A famous American politician of years ago made this prediction a few days before his death. He told a friend that when he was dead the American newspapers would say that a political boss was dead. But, he said, if he had lived the right kind of life under God, they would then have reported that there had come the death of a statesman. "Take warning by me," he counseled the young senator to whom he was talking. Then he rose on one elbow to write two words on the fly leaf of a book—"Dream true"; and he gave the book as a parting gift to the young senator.

"Dream true"—a nation and its leaders can dream true only when they live with the realization that there is an Almighty God who rules this earth and who chooses to rule through those appointed among men to carry the vast responsibilities of nations and peoples.

Or note the words that precede that verse chosen by President Eisenhower from the Thirty-third Psalm. "Let all the earth fear the Lord, let all the inhabitants of the world stand in awe of him! For he spoke, and it came to be; he com-

manded, and it stood forth. The Lord brings the counsel of
the nations to nought; he frustrates the plans of the peoples.
The counsel of the Lord stands for ever, the thoughts of his
heart to all generations." Then note the conclusion, "Blessed
is the nation whose God is the Lord."

No man can "dream true" who does not know and obey
the One who is "the Truth", Jesus Christ. It is He who has
unlocked the secrets of God's will, His power and love. For
this He came. And when the futile strivings of men after
right were most evident of all in their denial of His person,
He gave Himself to open up men's minds and hearts to God.
In this we see the greatness of His love. In this we see the
power which is His,—to recreate men's spirits, to refashion
men's lives, to remold their wills and ways.

"Dream true!"